food for

friends

food for
friends

hamlyn

First published in Great Britain in 1998 by
Hamlyn, a division of Octopus Publishing Group Limited
2–4 Heron Quays, London E14 4JP

Reprinted 2001

ISBN 0 600 60554 X

NOTES
Both metric and imperial measurements have been given in all
recipes. Use one set of measurements only, and not a mixture of
both.

Standard level spoon measurements are used in all recipes.
1 tablespoon = one 15 ml spoon
1 teaspoon = one 5 ml spoon

Eggs should be medium to large unless otherwise stated.
The Department of Health advises that eggs should not be
consumed raw. This book contains dishes made with raw or
lightly cooked eggs. It is prudent for more vulnerable people such
as pregnant and nursing mothers, invalids, the elderly, babies and
young children to avoid uncooked or lightly cooked dishes made
with eggs. Once prepared, these dishes should be kept refrigerated
and used promptly.

Meat and poultry should be cooked thoroughly. To test if poultry
is cooked, pierce the flesh through the thickest part with a skewer
or fork — the juices should run clear, never pink or red. Do not
re-freeze poultry that has been frozen previously and thawed.

Do not re-freeze a cooked dish that has been frozen previously.

Milk should be full fat unless otherwise stated.

Nut and Nut Derivatives
This book includes dishes made with nuts and nut derivatives. It
is advisable for customers with known allergic reactions to nuts
and nut derivatives and those who may be potentially vulnerable
to these allergies, such as pregnant and nursing mothers, invalids,
the elderly, babies and children to avoid dishes made with nuts
and nut oils. It is also prudent to check the labels of pre-prepared
ingredients for the possible inclusion of nut derivatives.

Pepper should be freshly ground black pepper unless otherwise
stated.

Fresh herbs should be used, unless otherwise stated. If
unavailable, use dried herbs as an alternative, but halve the
quantities stated.

Measurements for canned food have been given as a standard
metric equivalent.

Ovens should be pre-heated to the specified temperature– if using
a fan-assisted oven, follow the manufacturer's instructions for
adjusting the time and the temperature.

Vegetarians should look for the 'V' symbol on a cheese to
ensure it is made with vegetarian rennet. There are
vegetarian forms of Parmesan, feta, Cheddar, Cheshire, Red
Leicester, dolcelatte and many goats' cheeses, among others.

Contents

Introduction

Cooking for friends and family can be tremendous fun. Attitudes to entertaining have changed over the last few years and nowadays nobody expects the perfect performance from their host or hostess. But it is still important to plan the event in advance so that you are relaxed and well prepared and enjoy the occasion as much as your guests. This book aims to help you throw a successful party, whether it is a full-scale drinks party or a relaxed supper for a few close friends. With delicious recipes for every occasion, suggested menus and helpful advice on subjects such as setting the table, serving drinks, presenting, decorating and garnishing food and choosing wine and cheese, this book will prove invaluable, whatever the event.

What kind of event?

There are many different ways of entertaining, and the type of event you choose to host depends on a number of considerations. The most important are the number of people you wish to invite, the space you have available, how much crockery, cutlery and furniture you have, how much money you have to spend, and the time of year. The choice is endless. You might, for example, want to have a lavish dinner party for a few special friends; or you might prefer a less formal supper party for friends and family; or you might like to invite all the children and have a big family lunch. On the other hand, you might want to invite a larger crowd for a buffet party, which will give you the opportunity of entertaining more people than you can sit comfortably around a table. At the far end of the scale would be a large drinks and nibbles party, lasting only a couple of hours, but including virtually all your friends at once.

The type of event you choose will dictate the number of people you can comfortably accommodate. For a dinner party, eight people is about the maximum for most hosts or hostesses to contemplate, while the maximum number for a cocktail party or buffet is about 30, depending on the amount of space that there is available. Choosing what kind of event you have is the first decision you have to make.

Planning ahead

An impromptu party may sound like a great idea, but it rarely works in practice. The success of most parties relies on careful planning. It is a good idea to make a few lists to ensure you don't forget anything. A shopping list, a list of who you have invited and if there is anything they do not eat, a list of wine and other drinks you want to serve, and even a list of the things you need to do to get ready for the party. But the first thing is to plan what food and drinks you are going to serve. Follow the advice on pages 24–25, or choose one of the suggested menus on the following pages.

"Don't forget to allow time for setting and decorating the table..."

Setting the table

The way in which you lay your table is as much a reflection of your tastes and personality as the food you serve. For special parties, when you really want to impress, use the best you possess.

Entertaining is the perfect excuse to show off your most treasured china, cutlery, glasses and table linen, and it is the first impression that your guests will receive of the culinary pleasures to come. However formal or informal the occasion, take the effort to make sure the table looks just right and pay attention to every last detail. Make sure the glasses sparkle, the cutlery gleams and the flowers are fresh. Remember, too, that the overall style of the table should be in keeping with the occasion. For instance, a damask cloth and shining silver would be out of place for an informal supper, while a checked cloth would be inappropriate for a formal dinner with business colleagues.

Separate tables for children are a good idea if you are entertaining friends with children. The children enjoy the special treatment, and if you seat them around a coffee table, they can sit on cushions on the floor to minimize the chances of spillage and accidents.

When deciding what to serve, take into account how much time you are going to have for cooking. It is a good idea to make a rough plan, either on paper or in your head, of when you are going to cook or prepare various dishes, to check that your desired menu is actually feasible. Don't forget to allow time for setting and decorating the table, any emergency housework needed before the event, arranging flowers if you have them, making ice and chilling drinks, rearranging furniture and all those other little tasks that are necessary.

If you are planning an ambitious meal with several courses, you may even want to go as far as writing a schedule: when to switch the oven on, what food to start cooking when, when to cook the vegetables, when to take the dessert out of the freezer or the cheese out of the refrigerator, and so on.

"There is no easier way of making a table special than by dressing it with a well-chosen tablecloth or napkins. Napkins won't take up much room and give instant definition to each place setting."

Arranging cutlery and glasses

If you are organising a formal, five-course meal to impress, a typical place setting would work in the following way. The cutlery for the first course starts on the outside and you then work in towards the plate, finishing with the dessert cutlery. Therefore, on the right hand side, working from the outside, you will need: a bread or hors d'oeuvre knife, a soup spoon, a fish knife, a knife for the main course and lastly, the dessert spoon. On the left hand side, moving towards the plate, you will need an hors d'oeuvre fork, a fish fork, a fork for the main course and a dessert fork.

Wine glasses work in the opposite way and are used in order from the plate outwards, starting with a sherry glass, a white wine glass, red wine glass and lastly a dessert wine glass to accompany the dessert. A water glass can be placed behind the others.

An informal table setting, on the other hand, will automatically create a comfortable atmosphere, and put guests at their ease. The choice of cutlery depends on the food you are serving, but still arrange from the outside in, in order of course. Dessert spoons and forks can be placed, nose to tail, above the plate. Again, glasses should be used from the inside out, but it is normal to use fewer glasses at an informal occasion. A glass for wine and another for water is usually sufficient.

Napkins

Setting the table is about much more than arranging knives and forks. There is no easier way of making a table special than by dressing it with a well-chosen tablecloth or napkins, plain or fancy. Napkins are not only practical, they can also be stylish design elements. They offer great scope, from simple paper ones that are available in every conceivable colour, to elegant linen ones, plain or decorated, which can be imaginatively folded or simply laid on side plates. They won't take up much room on a crowded table, but will give instant definition to each place setting.

Seating people

You will probably have given some thought to who will get on with whom when you compiled your list of guests, so seating people shouldn't be a problem. People no longer tend to expect boy/girl/boy/girl arrangements, so seating plans don't need to be as contrived as they used to be. Do, however, try and avoid seating shy people next to one another as this can produce a weak link in the conversation around the table. It is also best to avoid seating people who work together, or who are in the same line of business together, if possible, as they may talk about work all evening.

Menu suggestions

There are, of course, endless combinations of dishes which would work well to form a memorable meal or buffet. Following are some suggestions which would work well on the occasions shown. You may have to adjust the quantities, depending on how many guests you have. With each of these menus, you could serve a cheeseboard either before or after the dessert and coffee to finish.

Dinner for two
Goats' Cheese in Vine Leaves *page 34*
Fragrant Baked Bream *page 42*
Tomato and Coriander Salad *page 173*
Iced Zabaione *page 118*

Informal supper for friends
Chillies Stuffed with Curried Crab *page 32*
Sauté of Chicken with Garlic, Lemon and Herbs *page 62*
Honey-glazed Turnips *page 110*
Banana Filo Pie *page 122*

Cook-ahead supper for friends
Courgette Fritters with Tzatziki *page 30*
Simple Beef Curry with Spinach *page 82*
Parsee Pilau Rice *page 100*
Pineapple Pavlova *page 125*

Special occasion dinner
Asparagus with Green Mayonnaise *page 28*
Spicy Mediterranean Prawns *page 55*
Duck in Port and Ginger Marinade *page 68*
Spinach with Olive Oil and Lemon Dressing *page 106*
Warm Espresso Chocolate Pots *page 126*
Exotic Ruby Fruit Salad with Cardamom *page 134*

Winter celebration meal
Mushroom Soup with Crispy Bacon *page 18*
Olive Focaccia *page 222*
Fillet Steak with Stilton and Croûtons *page 80*
Carrots with Ginger and Orange Butter *page 112*
Apple, Blackberry and Marmalade Crumble *page 128*

After-work supper
Walnut Orecchiette with Camembert
and Gruyère *page 94*
Exotic Ruby Fruit Salad with Cardamom *page 134*

Cook's Tools

Saucepans

It is well worth investing in the best saucepans you can afford. Good quality pans provide years of service, as well as producing better results when you are using them. Cheap pans are a false economy as they will soon burn and need to be replaced. Heavy-based stainless steel saucepans are the best for general use.

Steamer

A steamer set is ideal for cooking vegetables and fish, maintaining flavour and nutritional value.

Food processors

Electric food processors and blenders are invaluable for many jobs in the kitchen, taking the hard work out of chopping herbs, making cakes and pastry.

Mortar and pestle

A cup-shaped bowl and grinder used to grind spices to a fine powder or fresh herbs to a pulp for use in dressings or sauces.

Garlic press

Garlic presses are used to crush garlic cloves to a fine pulp to speed up cooking and release all the garlic flavour into the food.

Masher

Many vegetables can be mashed, not just potatoes. Try mashed carrot, swede, celeriac or any other root vegetables as an interesting accompaniment to meat, fish or vegetable courses.

Pasta spoon

The perfect utensil for serving pasta of all shapes and sizes, particularly long, thin pasta shapes such as spaghetti or tagliatelle which are hard to serve any other way.

Citrus juicer

Many recipes require lemon, lime or orange juice and freshly-squeezed juice is far superior to the juice you can buy in bottles. Juice squeezers make the job cleaner and easier.

Hand whisk

Perfect for whipping cream, beating eggs, and making batters, as well as stirring sauces as they thicken to remove any lumps that start to form.

Ice cream scoop

A rounded spoon used to make neat ice cream balls. Stand in warm water before use to make scooping easier.

Knives

If properly cared for, a good set of knives should last a lifetime. Knives come in all shapes and sizes, designed for different jobs. The bare essentials are a small, sharp paring knife for peeling and trimming vegetables; a large, wide-bladed chopping knife for preparing all sorts of ingredients including vegetables and meat; and a long serrated knife for slicing bread, cakes and pastry dishes. Clean and dry knives after use and keep them sharp to avoid unnecessary accidents and make them easier to use.

Palette knife

A flexible, wide-bladed knife which can be used for spreading cream, icing or fillings on cakes and in pies and tarts. When using with firm icings or toppings, warm the palette knife in a cup of hot water first to soften the icing and make spreading easier. Also useful for lifting small delicate cakes and pastries.

Vegetable peeler

As well as removing the peel from root vegetables, vegetable peelers are also invaluable for paring the rind from citrus fruits to use as an ingredient or a garnish, and can also be used for making Parmesan cheese shavings.

Melon baller

A small, rounded spoon that is used to scoop balls from a melon. This is one of the most attractive ways to serve melon.

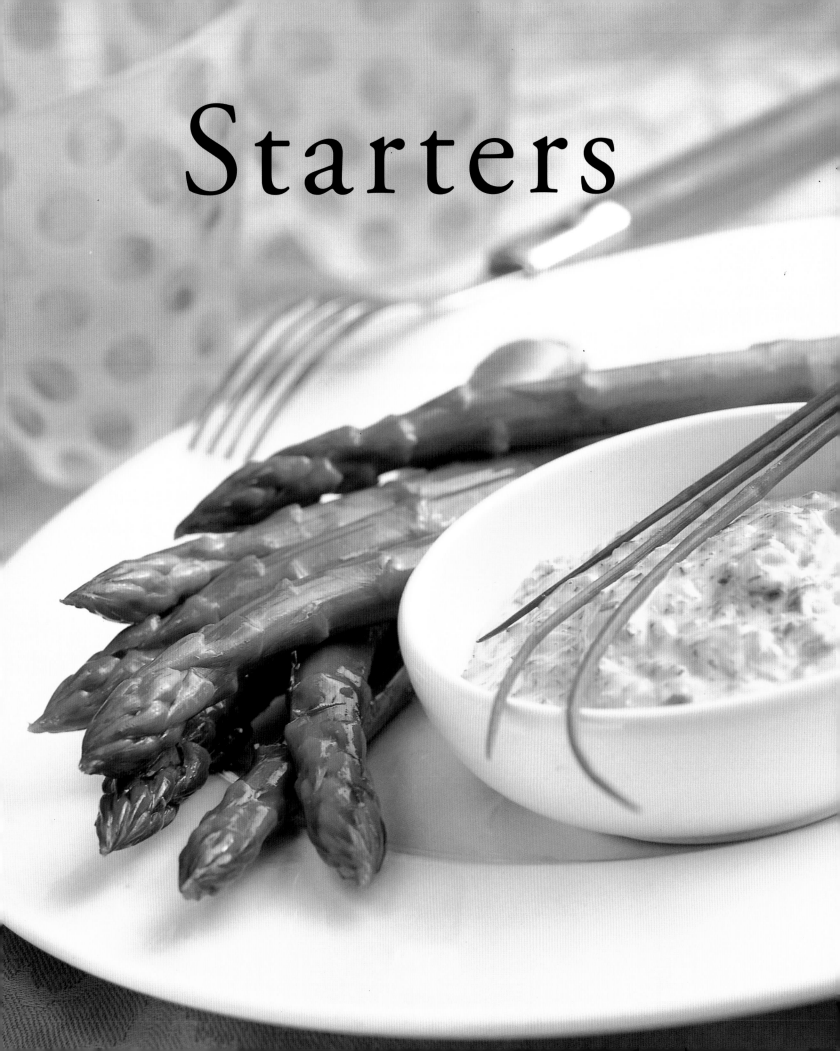

Starters

Sweet Red Pepper Soup

The Italian name for this soup is acquacotta con pepperoni, *which means 'cooked water'. Traditionally it included only a few vegetables boiled in water and poured over slices of stale bread.*

4 teaspoons olive oil

I red onion, finely chopped

2 celery sticks, finely sliced

2 red peppers, cored, deseeded and cut into very thin strips

2 plum tomatoes, roughly chopped

I garlic clove, crushed

I tablespoon plain flour

I litre/1¾ pints chicken or vegetable stock or water

I teaspoon sugar

2 eggs

4 thick slices of country bread

salt and pepper

chopped flat-leaf parsley, to garnish (optional)

heat the olive oil in a large heavy saucepan, add the red onion, celery and red peppers and cook gently, stirring frequently, for about 10 minutes until softened.

add the tomatoes, garlic and flour and stir well to mix. Cook for 1–2 minutes, stirring, then pour in the stock or water and bring to the boil. Add the sugar and salt and pepper to taste, half-cover and simmer gently for 30 minutes.

whisk the eggs in a bowl with salt and pepper to taste, then whisk in 1–2 ladlefuls of the hot soup. Pour this mixture into the pan of soup and heat very gently without boiling, stirring all the time. Taste for seasoning.

put a slice of bread in the bottom of 4 soup plates, ladle the soup over and garnish with parsley, if using. Serve hot.

Serves 4
Preparation time: *15 minutes*
Cooking time: *30 minutes*

clipboard: This soup is very good puréed, without the bread. Cook it for 40 minutes or until the pepper is very soft; work until smooth in a blender or food processor, then thicken with the eggs. For a smooth consistency, work the soup through a sieve to remove the pepper skins.

Mushroom Soup
with Crispy Bacon

50 g/2 oz butter

1 onion, finely chopped

1 garlic clove, finely chopped

375 g/12 oz mushrooms, finely sliced

2 tablespoons plain flour

600 ml/1 pint vegetable or chicken stock

150 ml/¼ pint milk

1 tablespoon Manzanilla sherry (optional)

150 ml/¼ pint whipping cream

4 rashers of bacon, rinded, cooked until crisp and cut into small pieces

salt and pepper

sprigs of chervil or parsley, to garnish

melt the butter in a large pan and fry the onion, garlic and mushrooms until soft and beginning to colour. Sprinkle on the flour and stir to combine. Gradually pour on the stock and milk, stirring well to blend. Bring to the boil, then reduce the heat and simmer for approximately 15–20 minutes.

add salt and pepper to taste, along with the sherry, if using, and half the cream. Reheat, then divide between 4–6 individual soup bowls. Whip the remaining cream until it is just holding its shape, then spoon a little on top of each bowl of soup. Sprinkle with the bacon pieces and garnish with a sprig of chervil or parsley.

Serves 4–6
Preparation time: *15 minutes*
Cooking time: *20 minutes*

clipboard: A mixture of cultivated and wild mushrooms gives the soup a special flavour. For a smooth soup, purée before adding the cream.

Watercress and Cucumber Soup

1 small onion, chopped
½ cucumber, diced
600 ml/1 pint chicken stock
1 bunch of watercress
2 teaspoons lemon juice
good pinch of ground coriander
300 ml/½ pint milk
2 teaspoons cornflour
salt and pepper

put the onion, cucumber and chicken stock into a saucepan and bring to the boil. Cover and simmer for 15 minutes.

reserve a few sprigs of watercress for the garnish and chop the remainder. Add the chopped watercress, lemon juice, and coriander to the saucepan, season to taste with salt and pepper, cover and simmer for a further 10 minutes.

cool slightly, then purée, liquidize or sieve the soup. Return to a clean pan, add the milk and bring back to the boil.

blend the cornflour with a little cold water, add to the soup and bring back to the boil again. Simmer for 2 minutes, then adjust the seasonings. Serve garnished with the reserved watercress sprigs.

Serves 4
Preparation time: *15 minutes*
Cooking time: *35 minutes*

clipboard: This soup is also good served cold as a summer time first course. Make it the day before it is to be served and keep it covered in the refrigerator.

Moroccan Fish Soup

3 tablespoons olive oil

2 onions, chopped

2 celery sticks, sliced

4 garlic cloves, crushed

I fresh chilli, deseeded and finely chopped

½ teaspoon ground cumin

I cinnamon stick

½ teaspoon ground coriander

2 large potatoes, chopped

1.5 litres/2½ pints fish stock or water

3 tablespoons lemon juice

large bunch of mixed herbs, including dill, parsley and coriander, chopped

2 kg/4 lb mixed fish and shellfish, prepared

4 well-flavoured tomatoes, skinned, deseeded and chopped

salt and pepper

heat the oil in a large saucepan. Add the onion and celery and fry gently for about 10–15 minutes until softened and transparent, adding the garlic and chilli towards the end. Add the cumin, cinnamon and ground coriander and stir for 1 minute, then add the potatoes and cook, stirring, for a further 2 minutes.

add the stock or water and the lemon juice. Heat to simmering point, then simmer gently, uncovered, for about 20 minutes until the potatoes are tender.

reserve a tablespoon of the herbs, then add the remainder with the fish, shellfish, and tomatoes. Season with salt and pepper, and cook gently for another 10–15 minutes until the fish and shellfish are tender. Serve immediately, garnished with the reserved chopped herbs.

Serves 6–8
Preparation time: *20 minutes*
Cooking time: *about 45 minutes*

clipboard: Any selection of fish and shellfish can be used for this recipe, except oily fish like mackerel and sardines. The trimmings, heads, tails, bones and shells can all be used to make the fish stock.

Menu Planning

Most people find that planning the menu for a party is great fun and it certainly allows you to use your creativity. The dishes you choose will depend on what type of party you are throwing, for example, whether it is a dinner party or a buffet, the time of year and the tastes of your guests. Unless it is a very special occasion, it is a good idea to limit the number of courses to three, or four if you are serving cheese, and coffee afterwards. Choose one really spectacular course to impress everyone and keep the rest simple. For a drinks and nibbles party, choose six to eight different dishes, and when planning a barbecue, choose three or four main courses and serve with bread and a variety of salads, followed by a simple dessert. However well you plan, there never seems to be as much time as you think

there will be, so don't make it difficult for yourself. Always aim for variety when planning a menu; variety in flavour, colour, texture and even shape. Just as you wouldn't serve lemon chicken followed by lemon mousse, so you shouldn't choose a succession of bright orange dishes, or a savoury mousse followed by a sweet mousse, or more than one course with a crunchy texture. If you have trouble choosing, there are a number of menus for different occasions in the Introduction. Whatever dishes you choose, it is nice to display the menu at the table for your guests to peruse. This will let them know what they are eating and what to expect for the rest of the meal. Write it out clearly on coloured card or handmade paper to co-ordinate with the rest of your table setting.

Curried Sweetcorn Patties

These patties are an ideal starter for a dinner party or can be eaten as a light lunch snack.

375 g/12 oz sweetcorn kernels
2 tablespoons cornflour, sieved
2 tablespoons plain flour, sieved
1 egg, lightly beaten
¼ teaspoon salt
1 teaspoon curry powder
½ teaspoon chilli powder
¼ teaspoon turmeric
1 shallot, very finely chopped
2 tablespoons chopped fresh coriander
oil, for deep-frying

Yogurt dip
4 tablespoons natural yogurt
1 tablespoon lemon juice
1 tablespoon chopped fresh coriander
1 teaspoon clear honey
¼ teaspoon garam masala
¼ teaspoon salt

To garnish
lemon wedges
few sprigs of coriander

reserve 4 tablespoons of the sweetcorn. Place the remaining corn in a food processor or blender with the cornflour, plain flour, egg, salt, curry powder, chilli powder and turmeric. Blend briefly to combine the ingredients (the corn should be slightly broken up), then transfer the mixture to a bowl and stir in the shallot, coriander and reserved sweetcorn.

heat the oil in a saucepan for deep-frying to 190°C/375°F, or until a cube of bread browns in 30 seconds. Drop dessertspoonfuls of the corn mixture into the hot oil and cook the patties in batches for 3–4 minutes per batch until they are crisp and golden. Remove with a slotted spoon and drain on kitchen paper.

mix together all the ingredients for the yogurt dip, taste and adjust the seasoning if necessary. Serve the patties hot, with the yogurt dip, garnished with the lemon wedges and coriander.

Makes about 20 patties
Preparation time: *20–30 minutes*
Cooking time: *15 minutes*

Asparagus
with Green Mayonnaise

2 bundles of asparagus
chives, to garnish

Green mayonnaise
3 egg yolks
1 tablespoon finely chopped chives
1 tablespoon finely chopped parsley
1 tablespoon lemon juice
300 ml/½ pint olive oil
salt and pepper

wash the asparagus and trim the ends. Scrape the lower half of each spear, then divide into 6 bunches.

tie each bunch firmly with string, finishing with a long-ended bow. (This makes it easier to remove the string after cooking.)

fill a large saucepan with salted water and bring to the boil. If you have a pan deep enough for the asparagus spears to stand upright, so much the better, as the tender points can then be above the water level. This means that they are steamed while the firmer parts of the stalks are actually boiling in the water.

place the lid on the pan, and boil until just tender. Do not overcook.

carefully remove the bunches and place them on a wire tray to drain and go cold.

to make the mayonnaise, place the egg yolks, herbs and lemon juice in a liquidizer or food processor and blend for 1–2 minutes. Keeping the motor running, pour in the oil in a very thin stream until it is all incorporated. Add salt and pepper to taste.

untie the bunches of asparagus and place 1 bunch on each plate. Serve the sauce separately, garnish with chives and accompany the dish with crusty bread.

Serves 6
Preparation time: *30 minutes*
Cooking time: *20–25 minutes*

Courgette Fritters
with Tzatziki

500 g/1 lb courgettes
25 g/1 oz polenta
25 g/1 oz plain flour
1 egg, lightly beaten
vegetable oil, for deep-frying
salt and pepper

Tzatziki

125 g/4 oz natural yogurt
1 garlic clove, crushed
1 tablespoon chopped mint
125 g/4 oz cucumber, peeled, grated and
squeezed dry

place all the ingredients for the tzatziki in a small bowl and stir well until evenly combined. Set aside for 30 minutes for the flavours to infuse.

cut the courgettes into thin slices about 5 mm/¼ inch thick. Mix the polenta and flour in a large bowl with plenty of salt and pepper. Dip the courgette slices, first into the egg and then into the polenta and flour to coat them evenly.

pour about 10 cm/4 inches of oil into a deep, heavy-based saucepan and heat to 190°C/375°F, or until a cube of bread browns in 30 seconds. Fry the courgette slices in batches for 2–3 minutes until crisp and golden. Drain on kitchen paper and serve hot with the tzatziki to dip.

Serves 4
Preparation time: *10 minutes,
plus chilling*
Cooking time: *2–3 minutes*

clipboard: The polenta, which is added to the flour coating on these thinly sliced courgettes, remains very crisp once cooked. The extra bite is quite delicious. Use half Greek yogurt and half natural yogurt for a creamier tzatziki. If wished, the fritters can be made in advance and reheated in a hot oven at 200°C/400°F/Gas Mark 6 for 10 minutes until crisped up.

Chillies Stuffed
with Curried Crab

Use jalapeño chillies for this recipe as they have thicker flesh than some chillies, making them easier to peel and stuff.

6 red jalapeño chillies

6 green jalapeño chillies

2 tablespoons vegetable oil

2 garlic cloves, crushed

1 teaspoon grated fresh root ginger

3 spring onions, chopped

2 kaffir lime leaves, very finely chopped

1 tablespoon Thai red curry paste

¼ teaspoon turmeric

150 g/5 oz fresh or canned white crab meat, flaked

1 tablespoon lime juice

2 teaspoons fish sauce (see page 58)

prepare the chillies for stuffing. Place them under a preheated hot grill and cook them, turning occasionally, until they have softened and their skins are patched with black. This will take about 8–10 minutes.

remove the chillies from the grill and leave them to cool, covered with sheets of dampened kitchen paper. (This will make them easier to peel once they have cooled.)

meanwhile prepare the stuffing. Heat the oil in a saucepan, add the garlic, ginger and spring onions and cook over a gentle heat for 3 minutes until softened. Stir in the lime leaves, red curry paste and turmeric and cook, stirring, for a further 2 minutes. Remove the pan from the heat and stir in the flaked crab, lime juice and fish sauce.

peel the chillies, leaving the stalks intact, and make a slit down one side of each chilli from the stalk to the tip. Scrape out and discard the seeds. Stuff the chillies with the curried crab mixture and place them in a shallow ovenproof dish and cover them with foil.

just before serving, place the chillies in a preheated oven, 200°C/400°F/Gas Mark 6, for 15 minutes, until they are heated through. Serve immediately.

Serves 4–6
Preparation time: *about 30 minutes*
Cooking time: *30 minutes*
Oven temperature: *200°C/400°F/Gas Mark 6*

Goats' Cheese
in Vine Leaves

*Goats' cheese is delicious when wrapped and grilled
in vine leaves. Choose small whole cheeses such as crottins
and serve the oozing cheese on toast with a salad or selection
of grilled vegetables.*

4–8 vine leaves, fresh or preserved in brine
1 tablespoon chopped thyme leaves
1 tablespoon chopped flat-leaf parsley
1 tablespoon chopped oregano
1 teaspoon crushed mixed peppercorns
1 tablespoon lemon juice
4 small whole goats' cheeses
2 tablespoons olive oil

if you are using vine leaves preserved in brine, rinse them well in a colander under cold running water. Bring a small saucepan of water to the boil, add the vine leaves and blanch for 1 minute. If using fresh vine leaves, remove any tough stems and blanch briefly in boiling water for 30 seconds. Regardless of type, refresh the blanched leaves under cold water, then drain well.

mix the chopped fresh herbs with the crushed peppercorns and lemon juice in a shallow bowl. Brush the goats' cheeses with olive oil and roll them in the herb mixture. Wrap the coated cheeses in the vine leaves, then brush them with any remaining olive oil.

place the wrapped goats' cheeses under a preheated hot grill or on an oiled barbecue grill over moderately hot coals. Cook for 8 minutes, turning once, until the cheeses are just soft. Serve with toasted crusty bread, salad or grilled vegetables, such as peppers.

Serves 4
Preparation time: *10 minutes*
Cooking time: *8 minutes*

Bruschetta
with Grilled Pepper and Hazelnuts

Bruschetta
4 thick slices of day-old rustic-style bread
2 garlic cloves, cut in half
extra virgin olive oil, to drizzle

Topping
1 yellow pepper, cored, deseeded and quartered
1 red pepper, cored, deseeded and quartered
2 tablespoons hazelnut oil
2 garlic cloves, sliced
1 tablespoon grated lemon rind
25 g/1 oz sultanas
25 g/1 oz flaked hazelnuts
175 g/6 oz salad leaves (such as
young spinach leaves, rocket, frisée)

make the topping: grill the pepper quarters, skin side up, for 6–8 minutes until charred and tender. Put into a plastic bag and set aside until cool enough to handle. Peel off the skin and slice the flesh.

heat the oil in a frying pan, add the garlic, lemon rind, sultanas and hazelnuts and fry gently for 5 minutes until golden. Add the salad leaves and cook over a low heat for 3 minutes, or until just wilted.

meanwhile prepare the bruschetta: toast the bread lightly on both sides, either over a barbecue or under a hot grill. Immediately rub the toast all over with the garlic cloves and drizzle with as much olive oil as liked.

divide the salad mixture between the bruschetta and top with the grilled peppers and the rest of the topping. Serve at once.

Serves 4
Preparation time: *7 minutes*
Cooking time: *15–20 minutes*

clipboard: To make the tomato and basil topping illustrated, place 4 quartered plum tomatoes in a roasting pan and drizzle with a little olive oil. Grill for about 10 minutes until golden. Spread 2 tablespoons of black olive paste over one side of each bruschetta and top with the tomatoes and basil leaves.

Risotto
with Sweet Pepper and Aubergine

2 tablespoons olive oil

40 g/1½ oz butter

1 shallot, finely chopped

1 aubergine, finely chopped

1 red pepper, cored, deseeded and finely diced

1 litre/1¾ pints vegetable stock

375 g/12 oz arborio rice

50 ml/2 fl oz dry white wine

1 tablespoon chopped parsley

4 basil leaves, finely chopped

25 g/1 oz Parmesan cheese shavings

2 tablespoons single cream

salt and pepper

heat the oil and all but 1 tablespoon of the butter in a deep pan. Add the shallot and fry over a medium heat for a few minutes until golden, but not brown. Add the aubergine to the pan with the diced pepper. Cook for about 5 minutes on a fairly high heat. Meanwhile put the stock in another pan over a medium heat and slowly bring to the boil.

add the rice to the vegetable mixture, stir for a few minutes, then add the wine. When this has evaporated pour in a little of the boiling stock. Continue adding the stock in small amounts, stirring frequently, for about 25 minutes, until the rice is creamy and the stock has been absorbed.

taste and adjust the seasoning, if necessary. Add the reserved butter, chopped herbs, Parmesan and cream. Mix well and serve.

Serves 4
Preparation time: *5–10 minutes*
Cooking time: *35 minutes*

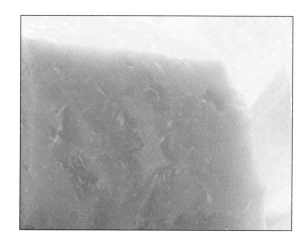

Fish

Fragrant Baked Bream

Sea bream is a delicious, delicately flavoured fish, which absorbs the flavours of these spices to perfection.

1 tablespoon flaked almonds, lightly toasted and chopped
1 teaspoon paprika
1 teaspoon ground cinnamon
2 teaspoons ground cumin
pinch of crushed saffron threads
½ teaspoon cayenne pepper
2 garlic cloves, crushed
2 teaspoons caster sugar
750 g/1½ lb sea bream, prepared
3 tablespoons lemon juice
4 tablespoons olive oil
salt and pepper

To serve
flat-leaf parsley
2 tomatoes, sliced

mix together the almonds, paprika, cinnamon, cumin, saffron, cayenne pepper, garlic and sugar. Season with salt and pepper. Cut 3 slashes in both sides of the sea bream. Rub the spice mixture over the fish, working it well into the slashes. Pour the lemon juice and olive oil over the fish. Cover and leave in a cool place for 1 hour.

put the fish and any marinade in a shallow earthenware baking dish. Cover with foil and bake in a preheated oven, 180°C/350°F/Gas Mark 4, for about 20–25 minutes, until the flesh flakes when tested with a fork.

serve on a bed of flat-leaf parsley and tomato slices.

Serves 2
Preparation time: *20 minutes, plus marinating*
Cooking time: *20–25 minutes*
Oven temperature: *180°C/350°F/Gas Mark 4*

clipboard: Saffron threads are the dried stigmas of a species of crocus called the *Crocus sativus*. Each stigma must be picked by hand, a delicate job indeed. Since it takes over 4,000 crocus flowers to yield just 25 g/1 oz of saffron, its price is even greater than its weight in gold. Yet such is its potency that even a few threads can dramatically change the flavour and colour of a dish.

Red Mullet
with Fennel and Rouille

6 medium red mullet, filleted
2 tablespoons olive oil
2 small fennel bulbs, finely sliced
salt and pepper

Rouille
3 garlic cloves, peeled
1–2 fresh red chillies, deseeded and coarsely chopped
2 egg yolks
175–250 ml/6–8 fl oz olive oil
lemon juice (optional)

rinse the red mullet fillets and pat dry. Brush the fish with a little oil, then wrap the fillets around the fennel slices. Put them on a baking sheet lined with greased aluminium foil and bake in a preheated oven, 180°C/350°F/Gas Mark 4, for 20 minutes, or until cooked.

make the rouille: pound the garlic thoroughly using a pestle and mortar. Add the chillies and pound to a paste. Whisk the egg yolks in a large bowl, then whisk into the garlic paste, mixing thoroughly.

add a few drops of olive oil, beating well, then a few more once the first have been absorbed. Continue adding the oil, a little at a time, as if making mayonnaise, beating constantly and adding more oil only when the previous addition has been amalgamated. The mixture will be very thick, and a deep pink colour. Season with salt and pepper to taste, and add a few drops of lemon juice, if liked. Serve the mullet and fennel accompanied by the rouille and green beans, if liked.

Serves 6
Preparation time: *20 minutes*
Cooking time: *20 minutes*
Oven temperature: *180°C/350°F/Gas Mark 4*

clipboard: This recipe is ideal for a dinner party because so much of the preparation can be done in advance. The mullet may be prepared up to 1 hour ahead, covered and kept in a cool place. The rouille can be made up to 24 hours in advance, covered and kept chilled, in which case use only 1 chilli otherwise the flavour will become too hot.

Tuna Livorno-Style

4 tuna steaks
50 g/2 oz plain flour
4 tablespoons olive oil
I small onion, finely chopped
4 parsley sprigs, finely chopped
125 ml/4 fl oz dry white wine
I tablespoon capers, drained
I bay leaf, crumbled
¼ teaspoon ground cinnamon
salt and pepper

coat the tuna steaks in flour. Heat the oil in a large heavy-based frying pan; mix together the onion and parsley and add them to the pan. Sauté over a moderate heat, stirring, until just golden but not brown.

add the tuna steaks and cook for 2 minutes on each side. Season with salt and pepper and add the wine. Leave until the wine has evaporated a little, then add the capers, crumbled bay leaf and cinnamon. Cover and cook for 15 minutes, adding water if needed.

serve the tuna steaks with the cooking juices poured over, accompanied by new potatoes and a green salad, if liked.

Serves 4
Preparation time: *5 minutes*
Cooking time: *25 minutes*

clipboard: Capers are the small unopened flower buds of a Mediterranean plant. They are usually pickled in vinegar and add a touch of piquancy to sauces, dressings and salads. They go especially well with fish.

Mixed Seafood Tagine

This dish hails from Morocco, where it is usual to use the best fresh fish available.

750 g/1½ lb mussels, thoroughly cleaned

1 onion, finely chopped

250 ml/8 fl oz fish stock

2 ripe well-flavoured tomatoes, seeded and chopped

2–3 garlic cloves, finely sliced

¼ teaspoon ground cardamom

¼ teaspoon ground cumin

¼ teaspoon ground coriander

large pinch of ground allspice

large pinch of ground turmeric

250 g/8 oz squid, prepared and cut into pieces

250 g/8 oz large raw prawns, peeled

salt and cayenne pepper

sprigs of coriander, to garnish

discard any mussels that are open, then put the mussels, onion and stock into a large saucepan. Cover and cook over a medium heat, shaking the pan occasionally, for 3–5 minutes, depending on the size of the mussels, until they have all opened. Discard any mussels that remain closed. Leave to cool before removing the mussels from their shells. Set aside.

strain the cooking liquid into a bowl, leave to stand for 2–3 minutes, then carefully strain most of it into a large heavy-based frying pan, leaving behind any sediment and onion.

add the tomatoes, garlic, cardamom, cumin, coriander, allspice and turmeric to the frying pan. Bring to the boil, then simmer gently for about 5 minutes until the garlic is tender.

add the squid to the frying pan, cover and poach for 1 minute until the pieces of squid curl up. Add the prawns, cover the pan and continue to cook gently for 1 minute. Add the mussels, season with salt and cayenne pepper, and cook for 1 minute further to heat through. Serve at once, garnished with the sprigs of coriander.

Serves 4
Preparation time: *20 minutes*
Cooking time: *20–25 minutes*

clipboard: A tagine is a deep earthenware dish with a conical lid, used throughout North Africa to make all sorts of stews. The food cooked in it is also known as a tagine.

Swordfish
with Fennel Seeds

4 swordfish steaks, about 250 g/8 oz each
2 teaspoons fennel seeds, crushed
finely grated rind and juice of 1 lemon
1 tablespoon bottled capers, drained and chopped
2 tablespoons chopped dill
1 teaspoon paprika
1–2 garlic cloves, crushed
150 ml/¼ pint olive oil
dill sprigs or fennel fronds, to garnish

place the swordfish steaks in a single layer in a shallow dish. Mix the remaining ingredients in a jug, pour over the steaks and toss to coat well. Cover and marinate for 2–3 hours, turning the fish several times.

remove the fish from the dish using tongs. Pour the marinade into a jug. Cook the steaks under a preheated hot grill or on an oiled barbecue grill over hot coals for 5–7 minutes on each side, basting frequently with the marinade. Garnish with dill or fennel and serve with plain rice and salad or griddled fennel.

Serves 4
Preparation time: *10 minutes, plus
   marinating*
Cooking time: *10–15 minutes*

clipboard: Griddled fennel makes a delicious accompaniment to this dish. Cut 3 small fennel bulbs into quarters. Arrange the fennel on a preheated griddle pan and cook for about 8 minutes, turning twice, until softened and golden brown.

Al Fresco Dining

There is something magical about eating out of doors, whether it is at lunchtime under the shade of a spreading tree, or on a warm summer's evening by candlelight. If you have some outside space, whether it is a garden, patio or even just a balcony, it can be put to service as a delightful setting for a summer party al fresco. This could take the form of an intimate dinner for two, a small drinks party or a full-scale barbecue party, depending on just how much space you have. Outdoor meals require a different approach to table setting and dressing than meals indoors. Use brightly coloured table linen to show up in bright sunlight and choose fabrics you wouldn't dare use indoors, such as net, organza or silk. Take a more relaxed approach to co-ordinating and matching all the crockery and cutlery: a mismatched collection can look very effective in informal surroundings. And be more extravagant with the flowers to create a romantic setting. Consider decorating the table with huge vases or tiny posies of wild flowers, or sprinkle the cloth with rose petals or violets for the occasion. Make napkin rings out of twisted trails of ivy or clematis to complete the effect. If it is an evening party, use candles on the tables and lanterns in the trees to create a soft glow after dark. And from a more practical point of view, be ready to move the whole event inside at a moment's notice should the weather deteriorate just before or even during the meal. If it is windy, weigh down the edges of table cloths by wrapping small stones in the hem and holding them in place with ribbons. Another great idea for outside eating is a leisurely picnic which could take place in your own garden, in a park or woodland, or on the beach. All you need is a few drinks, some portable food and a picnic blanket or rug to sit on. See the Introduction for some menu suggestions for picnics and barbecues.

Spicy Mediterranean Prawns

Tiger prawns are delicious, if expensive, making this simple dish an absolute delight. It is very quick to prepare, so there should be no problem cooking this for friends after work.

500 g/1 lb raw tiger prawns, in their shells

4 tablespoons olive oil

2 garlic cloves, finely crushed

1 teaspoon ground cumin

¼ teaspoon ground ginger

1 teaspoon paprika

¼ teaspoon cayenne pepper

bunch of coriander, finely chopped

salt

lemon wedges, to serve

peel and devein most of the prawns, leaving a few whole since they look so attractive.

heat the olive oil in a frying pan, add the garlic and cook until it becomes aromatic. Stir in the cumin, ginger, paprika and cayenne pepper. Heat for about 30 seconds, then add the prawns. Fry quickly, stirring, until they turn pink. Stir in the coriander and season with salt.

heat for about 30 seconds, then serve the prawns with the cooking juices spooned over and accompanied by lemon wedges.

Serves 4
Preparation time: *10 minutes*
Cooking time: *about 3–4 minutes*

clipboard: These prawns can also be butterflied. Peel the prawns. Use scissors to cut them lengthways almost in half, leaving the tails intact. Marinate them in the fried spice mixture, then grill for 3–4 minutes. They can also be cooked on a barbecue in the summer.

Cod *with Black Beans and Ginger*

Fish steaks, laced with Chinese black beans and fragrant ginger, then steamed in foil parcels, make an unusual dish to be cooked on a barbecue or in the oven.

4 thick cod steaks, about 175 g/6 oz each

1 red chilli, deseeded and finely chopped

1½ tablespoons fermented black beans, finely chopped

2.5 cm/1 inch piece of fresh root ginger, peeled and finely chopped

finely grated rind and juice of 1 lime

1–2 tablespoons light soy sauce

2 garlic cloves, crushed

2 tablespoons rice wine or dry sherry

2 teaspoons sesame oil

2 spring onions, sliced

pepper, to taste

place the cod steaks in a single layer in a shallow dish. Mix together the remaining ingredients in a bowl. Pour the mixture over the fish, turning to coat. Cover and marinate for 30 minutes.

place each fish steak on a double square of foil. Turn up the edges of the foil slightly. Divide the marinade between the squares. Bring up the edges of the foil and press to seal.

cook in a preheated oven, 180°C/350°F/Gas Mark 4, for 10–15 minutes. The fish can also be cooked on a hot barbecue for the same length of time. Diners open their own parcels and mix the fragrant juices with plain rice or egg noodles and steamed vegetables.

Serves 4
Preparation time: *15 minutes, plus marinating*
Cooking time: *10–15 minutes*
Oven temperature: *180°C/350°F/Gas Mark 4*

clipboard: Fermented black beans are soya beans that have been salted and fermented. They are available from Oriental food stores and large supermarkets.

Cambodian Prawn Curry

Serve this fragrant curry with rice or bread.

3 tablespoons vegetable oil
300 ml/½ pint coconut milk
250 g/8 oz (prepared weight) young marrow, peeled, deseeded and cut into 2.5 cm/1 inch chunks
20 large raw prawns, peeled
2 tablespoons fish sauce
1 tablespoon lemon juice
1 teaspoon caster sugar
coriander sprigs, to garnish

Spice paste
1 onion, chopped
4 garlic cloves, chopped
1 lemon grass stalk, chopped
1 tablespoon chopped root ginger
2 teaspoons ground coriander
1 teaspoon chilli powder
½ teaspoon turmeric
½ teaspoon fennel seeds, lightly crushed

place all the ingredients for the spice paste in a blender or food processor and blend to a coarse paste. Heat the oil in a large flameproof casserole dish, add the spice paste and fry over a gentle heat, stirring, for about 8 minutes or until softened and aromatic.

add the coconut milk, stir well and simmer gently for 3–4 minutes. Stir the marrow into the sauce, cover the pan and cook gently for 5 minutes.

add the prawns, fish sauce, lemon juice and sugar to the casserole dish. Stir gently to combine all the ingredients and cook the curry, uncovered, for a further 5 minutes until the prawns have turned pink and are cooked through and the marrow is tender. Taste and adjust the seasoning, if necessary. Garnish with coriander sprigs and serve immediately.

Serves 4
Preparation time: *about 25 minutes*
Cooking time: *25 minutes*

clipboard: Fish sauce – properly known as *nam pla* – is a salty, spiced, fermented fish seasoning from Thailand. It is available from Oriental food stores and some supermarkets.

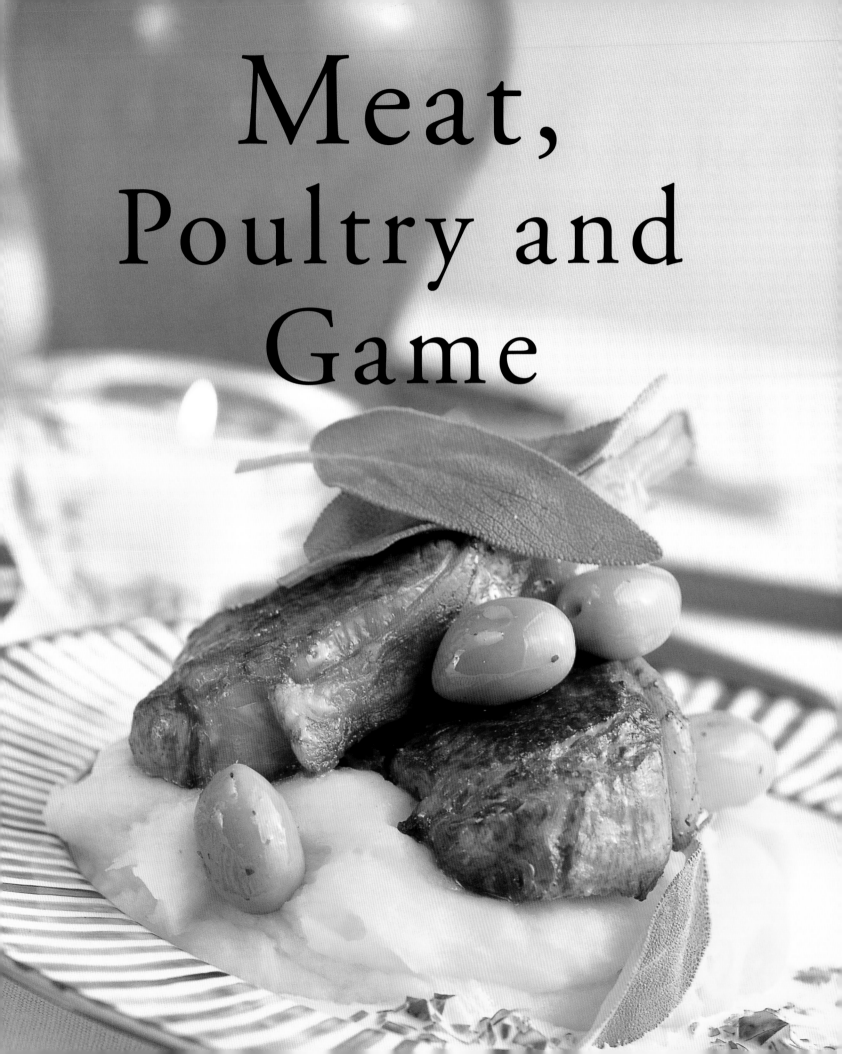

Meat, Poultry and Game

Sauté of Chicken
with Garlic, Lemon and Herbs

Lemon and fresh tarragon are perfect partners for this simple chicken dish.

4 tablespoons olive oil
2 garlic cloves, finely sliced
4 chicken portions
finely grated rind and juice of I lemon
I tablespoon chopped flat-leaf parsley
2 teaspoons chopped tarragon
salt and pepper

To garnish
lemon slices
sprigs of parsley and tarragon

heat the oil in a large, heavy-based saucepan and fry the garlic in the oil until lightly coloured but not browned.

add the chicken in a single layer. Season to taste and fry, turning frequently, for 15–20 minutes until the skin is crisp and golden brown.

lower the heat, cover the pan and continue cooking for 15–20 minutes until the juices run clear when the thickest part of the meat is pierced with a skewer or fork.

remove the chicken from the pan with a slotted spoon and place on a warm serving plate.

add the lemon rind and juice to the pan and stir well until sizzling to dislodge any sediment in the bottom of the pan.

remove from the heat and add the parsley and tarragon. Season with salt and pepper to taste. Stir well to mix, then pour the sauce over the chicken. Serve hot, garnished with lemon slices and sprigs of parsley and tarragon. A crisp green salad and French fries would make good accompaniments.

Serves 4
Preparation time: *10 minutes*
Cooking time: *30–40 minutes*

Chicken
with Olives and Lemon

A dish with a Moroccan flavour, it uses fresh rather than the traditional preserved lemons.

2 tablespoons olive oil
1 Spanish onion, finely chopped
3 garlic cloves
1 teaspoon ground ginger
1½ teaspoons ground cinnamon
large pinch of saffron threads, toasted and crushed
1 chicken, weighing about 1.75 kg (3½ lb)
750 ml (1¼ pints) chicken stock or water
125 g (4 oz) black or pink olives
1 large lemon, sliced
large bunch of coriander, finely chopped
large bunch of parsley, finely chopped
salt and pepper
flat-leaf parsley sprigs, to garnish

heat the oil, add the onion and fry gently, stirring frequently, until softened and golden.

meanwhile, in a mortar, crush the garlic with a pinch of salt, then work in the ginger, cinnamon, saffron and a little pepper. Stir into the onions, cook until fragrant, then remove from the pan and spread over the chicken.

put the chicken into a heavy-based saucepan or flameproof casserole that it just fits, add the stock or water and bring to simmering point. Cover and simmer very gently for about 1¼ hours, turning the chicken over 2–3 times.

add the olives, sliced lemon, coriander and parsley to the pan, cover and cook for 15 minutes or until the chicken is cooked through and tender. Transfer the chicken to a warmed serving dish, cover and keep warm. Boil the cooking juices to a rich sauce, adding salt and pepper to taste. Tilt the pan and skim off any surplus fat, if liked, then pour over the chicken and garnish with parsley.

Serves 4
Preparation time: *15 minutes*
Cooking time: *1¾ hours*

Chicken
with Oyster Mushrooms, Garlic and Cream

Oyster mushrooms are excellent in delicate creamy sauces such as this one.

125 g/4 oz rindless smoked streaky bacon rashers, cut into strips

15 g/½ oz butter

6 large skinless, boneless chicken breasts

1 tablespoon plain flour

300 ml/½ pint dry white wine

175 g/6 oz oyster mushrooms, finely sliced

1 garlic clove, crushed

75 ml/3 fl oz crème fraîche

½ teaspoon chopped rosemary, plus extra to garnish

salt and pepper

fry the strips of bacon gently in a large flameproof casserole dish, stirring, for about 5 minutes until the fat runs. Add the butter and, when melted, fry the chicken over a moderate heat for about 5 minutes until golden on all sides.

sprinkle in the flour and turn the chicken to coat, then gradually stir in the wine and bring to the boil, stirring constantly. Add the mushrooms, garlic and crème fraîche with the rosemary and plenty of pepper.

stir well, then cover and simmer gently for 25 minutes or until the chicken is tender when pierced with a skewer or fork. Turn and baste the chicken frequently.

taste the sauce and adjust the seasoning if necessary. Serve hot, garnished with rosemary. New potatoes tossed in chopped fresh herbs would go well with this dish, together with a crisp green salad.

Serves 6
Preparation time: *20 minutes*
Cooking time: *about 30 minutes*

Duck *in Port and Ginger Marinade*

This unusual combination of port and ginger with duck and fresh figs is magical — rich, luxurious and quite delicious.

2 kg/4 lb duck, cut into 8 pieces
1 onion, chopped
1–2 garlic cloves, crushed
500 ml/17 fl oz chicken stock
12 ripe figs
salt and pepper
chopped stem ginger, to garnish (optional)

Port and ginger marinade
400 ml/14 fl oz port
4 whole star anise
12 cm/5 inch piece of cinnamon stick
4 whole cloves
8 Szechuan or black peppercorns
2 tablespoons chopped stem ginger
4 tablespoons honey
piece of orange or tangerine peel
1 bay leaf
1 sprig of thyme

place the duck in a bowl, add the combined marinade ingredients, stir, cover and marinate in the refrigerator for at least 2 hours or overnight.

remove the duck from the marinade and pat dry. Heat a large flameproof casserole dish over a moderate heat; add the duck, a few pieces at a time, skin side down first, and brown well all over. Using a slotted spoon, transfer each batch to a colander to drain. Pour off most of the fat rendered from the duck, leaving about 1 tablespoon in the casserole dish.

add the onion and garlic to the casserole dish and cook gently for 5 minutes until softened. Return the duck pieces to the dish, pour in the marinade, bring to the boil and add the stock. Bring back to the boil, reduce the heat and season to taste. Cover with a tight-fitting lid and simmer gently for 45 minutes. Remove the lid, skim off any fat and lay the figs on top. Cover and cook for a further 20 minutes or until the meat and figs are just tender.

remove the meat and figs from the casserole and keep warm. Remove the star anise, cinnamon, bay leaf and thyme and set aside. Skim off as much fat as possible. Increase the heat and boil rapidly until the sauce is reduced by half; strain. Serve the duck with the sauce and the cooked figs. Use the reserved cinnamon, bay leaf and thyme and some chopped stem ginger to garnish, if liked.

Serves 4
Preparation time: *30 minutes, plus marinating*
Cooking time: *1½ hours*

Pigeon with Kumquats

3 tablespoons olive oil
6 young oven-ready pigeons
250 g/8 oz button onions, peeled
1 cinnamon stick
1 bay leaf
¾–1 teaspoon grated fresh root ginger
large pinch of saffron threads, toasted and crushed
900 ml/1½ pints chicken stock
250 g/8 oz kumquats, halved
2 tablespoons clear honey
salt and pepper
lightly toasted almonds, to garnish

heat the oil in a large, heavy-based flameproof casserole dish, add the pigeons in batches and cook until browned. Using a slotted spoon, transfer them to a dish. Stir the onions into the casserole and sauté until golden. Stir in the cinnamon, bay leaf, ginger, saffron and stock. Season with salt and pepper and bring to the boil.

return the pigeons to the casserole with any juices that have collected in the dish, cover and cook gently over a low heat, turning occasionally, for about 45 minutes, until they are tender.

add the kumquats and honey, cover and cook for a further 30–45 minutes until the pigeons are very tender. Using a slotted spoon, transfer them to a large warm serving dish, cover and keep warm.

boil the cooking liquid until slightly thickened. Taste and adjust the seasoning if necessary. Discard the cinnamon and bay leaf. Pour the sauce over the pigeons and scatter over the almonds.

Serves 6
Preparation time: *30 minutes*
Cooking time: *about 1½ hours*

clipboard: Kumquats are tiny egg-shaped fruits, rather like mini oranges. Native to China, they are now also grown in Florida and California. Unusually for a citrus fruit, the skin is sweeter than the flesh, which means that the whole fruit is eaten. If kumquats are not available, add 2 peeled and thickly sliced oranges to this recipe when the cooking liquid is almost reduced.

Food Presentation

Great presentation goes a long way towards making food enticing and this is vital when cooking for other people. Choose attractive plates and dishes in which to serve food, perhaps even consider making an ice bowl if serving ice cream, fruit salad or any other chilled dessert. A simple decoration or garnish will add a little extra something. Choose one that relates to the food.

Herbs

Most herbs have pretty leaves, particularly chervil, bay, sage, dill and parsley. Garnish a dish with a sprig of whatever herb has been used in it. Chopped herbs can be sprinkled over food.

Flowers

Edible flowers or petals can be used to decorate sweet and savoury foods. Chives, pot marigolds, primroses, violets and nasturtiums all make pretty decorations as well as tasty salad ingredients. They can be used fresh, or frosted with egg white and sugar.

Fruit

Many fruits are very pretty. Try raspberries, redcurrants or sliced strawberries to decorate summer cakes and desserts, or kiwi fruits and cape gooseberries for a change.

Citrus fruit

Orange, lemon and lime slices or wedges can add colour to sweet and savoury dishes. Pared rind also makes a great decoration. Remove the rind with a parer or cut off pieces with a vegetable peeler and cut into fine strips before use.

Vegetables

Many dishes look good served on a bed of salad leaves. Choose rocket for its distinctive taste and pretty shape, and lollo rosso for its frilly leaves, tinged with red. Whole or sliced chillies, and diced sweet peppers are also attractive. Courgette or carrot ribbons, made with a potato peeler, make an effective garnish.

Toasted seeds

Toasted sesame, pumpkin or sunflower seeds add flavour and texture to a dish and look great when sprinkled over the top.

Chocolate

Chocolate is good for decorating puddings and cakes. Use grated or melt it and drizzle over the top. It can also be melted and left to set on nonstick baking paper. You can then cut out shapes or make curls with a sharp knife.

Icing sugar

Use to dust sweet dishes and cakes for an effective finish.

Chicken *en Croûte*

2 tablespoons olive oil

125 g/4 oz brown cap mushrooms, finely chopped

2 garlic cloves, crushed

2 teaspoons chopped thyme

6 large skinless chicken breast fillets

125 g/4 oz pâté de campagne

2 tablespoons sherry or brandy

425 g/14 oz frozen puff pastry, thawed

salt and pepper

beaten egg, to glaze

Garnish

fried mushroom slices

sprigs of thyme

heat the oil in a small frying pan, add the mushrooms and fry over a moderate heat, stirring frequently, for about 5 minutes until the juices run. Increase the heat to high and stir the mushrooms until all of the liquid has evaporated and the mushrooms are quite dry. Add the garlic, thyme and salt and pepper to taste and cook for a further 5 minutes. Remove from the heat and leave to cool.

make a long horizontal slit through the thickest part of each chicken breast without cutting right through. Soften the pâté in a bowl with the sherry or brandy, then beat in the mushroom mixture until evenly combined. Spread the pâté inside the slits in the chicken breasts, dividing it equally between them, then close the chicken tightly around the stuffing.

roll out the pastry on a floured work surface and cut out 6 squares large enough to enclose the chicken breasts. Brush the edges of the pastry with water. Place a stuffed chicken breast in the centre of each pastry square, then fold the pastry around the chicken to form a parcel. Brush the seams with more water and press together well to seal.

put the chicken parcels, seam side down, on a moistened baking sheet. Roll out the pastry trimmings and cut small decorative shapes from it. Brush the parcels all over with beaten egg, then press the decorative shapes on top. Brush the shapes with beaten egg.

place in a preheated oven, 200°C/400°F/Gas Mark 6, for 30 minutes or until the pastry is golden brown and the chicken feels tender when pierced in the centre with a skewer. Serve hot, with green vegetables or ratatouille and garnish with a few fried mushroom slices and sprigs of thyme.

Serves 6
Preparation time: *30 minutes*
Cooking time: *about 40 minutes*
Oven temperature: *200°C/400°F/Gas Mark 6*

Duckling with Peppercorns

2 x 1 kg/2 lb oven-ready ducklings
25 g/1 oz butter
4 shallots, finely chopped
150 ml/¼ pint dry white wine
4 tablespoons brandy
4 tablespoons whole green peppercorns or
1 tablespoon black peppercorns, coarsely crushed
400 ml/14 fl oz double cream
salt and pepper
chervil, to garnish

prick the skins of the ducklings with a fork and season liberally with salt and pepper. Place in a roasting pan and roast in a preheated oven, 200°C/400°F/Gas Mark 6, for about 1¼ hours until tender.

meanwhile melt the butter in a pan, add the chopped shallots and cook until transparent. Stir in the white wine and brandy, bring to the boil and boil for 5 minutes.

cut the ducklings into pieces, arrange on a warm serving dish and keep hot. Add the peppercorns and cream to the sauce and season with salt to taste. Cook over a low heat for 3–5 minutes until thickened.

spoon the sauce over the ducklings and serve immediately, garnished with chervil. Green beans may be served as an accompaniment, if liked.

Serves 6
Preparation time: *20 minutes*
Cooking time: *1¼ hours*
Oven temperature: *200°C/400°F/Gas Mark 6*

clipboard: Duckling is a young duck, a bird which is highly esteemed by gourmets the world over. It is easily available from both butchers and supermarkets.

Breast of Pheasant
with Mustard Sauce

4–6 tablespoons butter
4 x 150 g/5 oz skinless, boneless pheasant breasts
salt and pepper

Sauce
300 ml/½ pint chicken or game stock
300 ml/½ pint red wine
2 tablespoons port
2–4 tablespoons wholegrain mustard
300 ml/½ pint single cream

To serve
425 g/14 oz Savoy cabbage, shredded
50 g/2 oz butter
chervil, to garnish

heat the butter in a large frying pan and cook the pheasant breasts over a gentle heat for 3–4 minutes. Turn and cook on the second side for a further 3–4 minutes. Remove from the heat, season with salt and pepper and leave to rest for 3 minutes before serving.

make the sauce by combining the stock, wine and port in a saucepan and simmering until reduced by half. Stir in the mustard and cream and simmer until the sauce thickens and coats the back of a spoon. Season to taste with salt and pepper.

boil the cabbage until just cooked, drain, toss in the butter and season with salt and pepper. Divide between 4 plates, piling it in the centre. Carve each pheasant breast into flat slices and arrange on top of the cabbage. Spoon a little sauce on each plate and garnish with chervil.

Serves 4
Preparation time: *10 minutes*
Cooking time: *10 minutes*

clipboard: Cooking times will vary depending on the thickness of the pheasant breast. When it is cooked, the flesh should feel firm but springy to the touch and when it is sliced, you can see it is only just cooked through.

Fillet Steak
with Stilton and Croûtons

As well as playing an important part on the cheeseboard, Stilton also has many uses in the kitchen. It is perfect in soup, scones and pies, as a topping for toasted bread, and it can also be used in stuffings for fillet of beef and breast of chicken.

125 g/4 oz Stilton
2 fillet steaks, about 4 cm/1½ inches thick
25 g/1 oz butter
15 g/1 oz croûtons
few thyme sprigs
watercress sprigs, to garnish
salt and pepper

trim the rind from the cheese and slice it until you have enough to cover the tops of the fillet steaks. Season the steaks with salt and pepper. Heat a little butter in a very hot pan and fry the steaks until sealed on both sides.

transfer to a buttered baking sheet and set the cheese on top. Put into a preheated oven, 220°C/425°F/Gas Mark 7, for 5 minutes for rare, 8 minutes for medium rare, and 15 minutes for well done, allowing the cheese to melt and colour lightly.

transfer the steaks to warm plates, scatter with the croûtons and sprigs of thyme and pour the cooking juices around the steaks. Garnish with sprigs of watercress. Serve immediately.

Serves 2
Preparation time: *5 minutes*
Cooking time: *5–15 minutes*
Oven temperature: *220°C/425°F/Gas Mark 7*

Simple Beef Curry *with Spinach*

If you would like to make this curry hotter, you can add some of the chilli seeds to it.

2 tablespoons ghee or vegetable oil
I large onion, finely sliced
2 garlic cloves, crushed
2 green chillies, deseeded and sliced
2 whole cloves, bruised
I teaspoon garam masala
I teaspoon ground coriander
I teaspoon turmeric
½ teaspoon chilli powder
I½ teaspoons ground cumin
625 g/I¼ lb beef fillet, cut into bite-sized pieces
I teaspoon salt
175 g/6 oz tomatoes, cut into large dice
150 ml/¼ pint coconut milk
250 g/8 oz young leaf spinach
I teaspoon lemon juice

heat the ghee or oil in a saucepan, add the onion and garlic and fry over a gentle heat, stirring frequently, for about 5 minutes or until softened. Stir in the chillies and fry for a further 2 minutes.

add the cloves, garam masala, coriander, turmeric, chilli powder and cumin. Stir well to mix and fry, stirring constantly, for 2 minutes.

stir in the beef and salt and cook, stirring, for 3 minutes to seal the meat, then add the tomatoes, coconut milk and spinach and stir to mix. Cover and simmer gently, stirring occasionally, for 20 minutes.

stir in the lemon juice and cook the curry, uncovered, for a further 8–10 minutes, stirring occasionally, until the sauce has thickened. Taste and adjust the seasoning, if necessary, and serve immediately.

Serves 4
Preparation time: *about 20 minutes*
Cooking time: *35–40 minutes*

clipboard: You can also make this curry using bite-sized pieces of lamb fillet instead of beef. Cook for the same length of time.

Roast Fillet of Lamb *with Wild Mushrooms*

1 lamb fillet, about 500 g/1 lb, trimmed to leave only a thin layer of fat on one side

vegetable oil, for frying

1 small green cabbage, finely shredded

125 g/4 oz butter

125 g/4 oz unsmoked back bacon, diced

175 g/6 oz mixed wild mushrooms, sliced if large

50 ml/2 fl oz red wine

2 tablespoons port

salt and pepper

chervil or parsley sprigs, to garnish

cut the lamb into 4 pieces and season well with salt and pepper. Heat the oil in a roasting pan and fry the lamb until sealed on all sides. Put the lamb in a preheated oven, 220°C/425°F/Gas Mark 7, and roast for 10–12 minutes for medium rare lamb, 15 minutes for medium, and 20 minutes for well done. Remove from the oven and keep warm.

boil the cabbage while the lamb is cooking, until it is tender, then drain, toss in half the butter, season with salt and pepper and keep warm. Fry the bacon in the remaining butter until lightly browned, add the mushrooms and fry for 2–3 minutes. Keep warm.

discard the fat from the roasting pan and pour in the wine and port. Bring to the boil on top of the stove, stirring continuously. Pour over the mushrooms and bacon, and season with salt and pepper to taste.

divide the cabbage between 4 warm serving plates, piling it in the centre of each plate. Cut each piece of lamb in half and arrange on top of the cabbage. Scatter the mushrooms, bacon and a little of the wine sauce around the edge. Garnish with chervil or parsley and serve immediately.

Serves 4
Preparation time: *30 minutes*
Cooking time: *10–20 minutes*
Oven temperature: *220°C/425°F/Gas Mark 7*

Lamb Cutlets
with Sherry Sauce

Sherry immediately adds a rich depth of flavour to a dish, without the need for lengthy cooking.

8 lamb cutlets
1 garlic clove, sliced
1–2 tablespoons oil
25 g/1 oz unsalted butter
1 tablespoon chopped thyme
1 tablespoon chopped parsley
1 tablespoon chopped sage
1 tablespoon chopped chives
150 ml/¼ pint dry sherry
150 ml/5 fl oz double cream
salt and pepper

To garnish
125 g/4 oz green olives, pitted
sage leaves

cut small slits in the lamb cutlets and push in the garlic slices. Heat the oil and butter in a frying pan, add the cutlets and brown on both sides. Lower the heat and cook for 6 minutes on each side.

remove from the frying pan with a slotted spoon and drain on kitchen paper. Arrange on a warm serving dish and keep warm.

add the herbs and sherry to the pan and boil rapidly for 2 minutes, until thickened. Stir in the cream, and season with salt and pepper to taste.

spoon the sauce over the cutlets and serve immediately, garnished with olives and sage.

Serves 4
Preparation time: *10 minutes*
Cooking time: *15 minutes*

clipboard: Olives – both green and black – are excellent for garnishing. They are good in breads, too, and chopped olives can also be used in stuffings, pasta or potato salads and pizza toppings.

Pork Fillet
with Rosemary and Fennel

Rosemary and fennel make a wonderful combination, which marries well with the pork fillet.

750 g/1½ lb pork fillet, trimmed of any fat
few rosemary sprigs, broken into small pieces
3 garlic cloves, sliced lengthways
4 tablespoons olive oil
2 fennel bulbs
300 ml/½ pint white wine
150 g/5 oz mascarpone cheese
salt and pepper

pierce the pork with a sharp knife blade and insert small sprigs of rosemary and slices of garlic evenly all over the fillet.

heat 2 tablespoons of olive oil in a frying pan, add the pork fillet and fry for 5 minutes or until browned.

trim the fennel, cut it into wedges and remove the solid central core. Lightly oil a roasting pan, place the trimmed fennel in it and drizzle with the remaining olive oil. Place the fillet on top and season with salt and pepper. Place in a preheated oven, 230°C/450°F/Gas Mark 8, and roast for 25 minutes.

add the wine to the frying pan in which the pork was fried and simmer, to reduce by half. Add the mascarpone cheese, season to taste, and stir to mix well.

serve the pork in slices with the wedges of fennel. Pour the sauce into the roasting pan and simmer over a low heat on top of the stove until slightly thickened. Stir well and spoon over the pork and fennel.

Serves 2
Preparation time: *15 minutes*
Cooking time: *30 minutes*
Oven temperature: *230°C/450°F/Gas Mark 8*

Beef Braised in Red Wine

1.5 kg/3 lb joint of topside or rolled silverside
25 g/1 oz bacon fat or dripping
1 onion, finely chopped
1 rosemary sprig
salt and pepper

Marinade
1 onion, sliced
1 carrot, sliced
1 celery stick, sliced
2 garlic cloves, crushed
2 bay leaves
6 peppercorns
600 ml/1 pint red wine

To garnish
rosemary sprigs
rocket leaves

start by marinating the beef. Put the meat in a deep bowl and add the marinade ingredients. Cover the bowl and place in the refrigerator to marinate for 24 hours, turning the beef several times. Lift the meat out of the marinade and dry it carefully. Reserve the marinade.

heat the bacon fat or dripping in a large flameproof casserole dish and sauté the chopped onion over a low heat for about 5 minutes, or until it is soft and golden. Add the beef, increase the heat and brown quickly on all sides.

strain the reserved marinade into the casserole dish and bring to the boil. Add the rosemary and season with salt and pepper. Lower the heat, cover tightly and simmer gently for at least 3 hours, or until the meat is tender. Turn the meat once halfway through cooking.

transfer the meat to a carving dish or board and slice fairly thickly. Arrange the slices on a warm serving dish. If the sauce is too thin, reduce a little by rapid boiling. Remove the rosemary and pour the sauce over the meat. Garnish with rosemary sprigs and rocket leaves and serve immediately on a bed of noodles, if liked.

Serves 6
Preparation time: *10 minutes, plus marinating*
Cooking time: *3½ hours*

clipboard: Marinating beef tenderizes it as well as imparting all the flavours of the marinade.

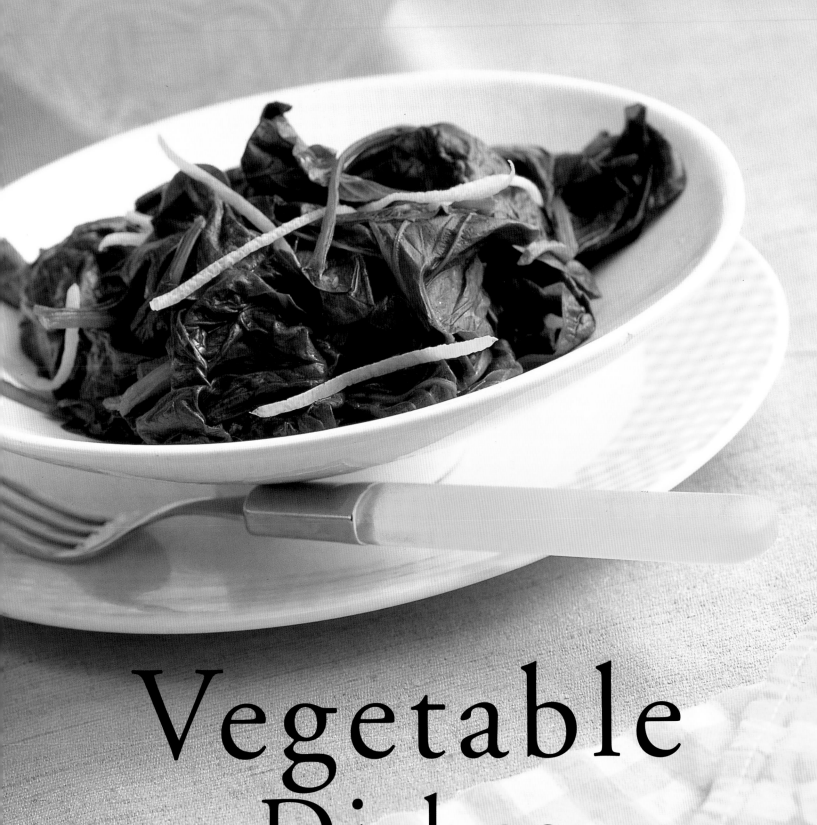

Vegetable
Dishes

Walnut Orecchiette *with Camembert and Gruyère*

4 tablespoons olive oil
300 g/10 oz dried orecchiette
2 garlic cloves, crushed
125 g/4 oz walnut pieces
2 plum tomatoes, cut into wedges
50 g/2 oz Camembert cheese
50 g/2 oz Gruyère cheese
1 bunch of chives, snipped
salt

bring at least 1.8 litres/3 pints of lightly salted water to the boil in a large saucepan. Add a dash of oil and cook the pasta for about 8–10 minutes, until just tender.

drain the pasta, then set it aside. Heat the remaining oil in a large saucepan, add the garlic, walnuts and tomatoes and fry for 1 minute, stirring. Add the drained pasta to the walnut sauce and toss well. Reduce the heat.

cut the Camembert into chunks, and grate the Gruyère. Add both cheeses to the sauce, followed by all except 2 tablespoons of the snipped chives. Toss well, spoon on to warm plates and garnish with the reserved snipped chives.

Serves 4
Preparation time: *10 minutes*
Cooking time: *15 minutes*

clipboard: Orecchiette means, literally, 'little ears' and is the name of this type of pasta which is, not surprisingly, ear-shaped. Cheeses play an important part not only on the cheeseboard but also in the cook's array of flavourings that can be used during the cooking process. Gruyère and Camembert are both well-known French cheeses and are excellent when used in sauces.

Vegetable Biryani

A biryani is an Indian rice dish made with either meat or vegetables, or a combination of both. This vegetarian dish makes an excellent meal in itself.

250 g/8 oz basmati rice, rinsed
6 tablespoons sunflower oil
2 large onions, finely sliced
2 garlic cloves, crushed
2 teaspoons grated root ginger
250 g/8 oz sweet potato, diced
2 large carrots, diced
1 tablespoon curry paste
2 teaspoons ground turmeric
1 teaspoon ground cinnamon
1 teaspoon chilli powder
300 ml/½ pint vegetable stock
4 ripe tomatoes, skinned, seeded and diced
175 g/6 oz cauliflower florets
125 g/4 oz frozen peas, thawed
50 g/2 oz cashew nuts, toasted
2 tablespoons chopped fresh coriander
salt and pepper
2 hard-boiled eggs, quartered, to serve

bring a large saucepan of salted water to the boil, add the basmati rice and return to a simmer. Cook gently for 5 minutes. Drain, refresh under cold water and drain again. Spread the rice out on a large baking sheet and set aside to dry.

heat 2 tablespoons of the oil in a frying pan, add half the onion and fry over a medium heat for 10 minutes until very crisp and golden. Remove with a slotted spoon and drain on kitchen paper. Reserve for garnishing.

add the remaining oil to the pan and fry the remaining onion with the garlic and ginger for 5 minutes. Add the sweet potato, carrot and spices and continue to fry for 10 minutes until light golden.

add the stock and tomatoes, bring to the boil, cover and simmer gently for 20 minutes. Add the cauliflower and peas and cook for a further 8–10 minutes until all the vegetables are tender.

stir in the rice, cashew nuts and coriander. Cook, stirring, for 3 minutes, then cover and remove from the heat. Check and adjust the seasoning if necessary. Leave to rest for 5 minutes before serving. Garnish with the crispy onions and egg quarters.

Serves 4
Preparation time: *25 minutes*
Cooking time: *50–55 minutes*

Chicory Salad

This attractive side salad is good with plain grilled or barbecued fish or meat.

2 chicory heads
4 tablespoons olive oil
125 g/4 oz pancetta, finely diced
125 g/4 oz pecorino cheese, grated
1 tablespoon lemon juice
pepper

separate the chicory leaves and wash and dry them carefully. Arrange them, rounded-side down, on a large serving platter.

heat 1 tablespoon of the oil in a non-stick frying pan. Add the pancetta and cook over a low heat until the fat runs. Increase the heat to medium and cook, stirring constantly, until the pancetta begins to colour and crisp. Remove the pan from the heat and transfer the pancetta to kitchen paper with a slotted spoon. Let the pancetta drain.

sprinkle the pancetta inside the chicory leaves, then sprinkle over the pecorino and pepper to taste.

add the remaining oil and the lemon juice to the pan juices and return the pan to a medium heat. Stir until sizzling, then drizzle over the chicory. Serve immediately.

Serves 4
Preparation time: *10 minutes*
Cooking time: *about 5 minutes*

clipboard: Pancetta is a type of cured pork that looks and tastes like bacon. If unavailable, you can use unsmoked streaky bacon rashers instead.

Parsee Pilau Rice

This traditional rice dish goes particularly well with the beef curry on page 82.

2 tablespoons ghee or butter

6 cardamom pods, bruised

5 whole cloves

7 cm/3 inch piece of cinnamon stick, broken in half

¼ teaspoon black peppercorns, lightly crushed

¼ teaspoon saffron threads

375 g/12 oz basmati rice

¾ teaspoon salt

½ teaspoon orange-flower water (optional)

25 g/1 oz sultanas

25 g/1 oz roasted cashew nuts

25 g/1 oz pistachio nuts

heat the ghee or butter in a large, heavy-based saucepan. Stir in the cardamom pods, cloves, cinnamon stick and peppercorns, and fry over a gentle heat, stirring constantly, for 2 minutes until fragrant. Add the saffron threads and rice to the pan and fry, stirring constantly, for 1 minute further.

add the salt, orange-flower water, if using, and 600 ml/1 pint water. Stir well to mix. Bring to the boil, then reduce the heat, cover the pan and cook the rice over a moderate heat for 15 minutes without removing the lid.

remove the pan from the heat and lightly loosen the rice grains with a fork. (All the water should have been absorbed.) Stir the sultanas into the rice, cover the pan with a clean, dry tea towel and allow the rice to cook in its own heat for a further 5 minutes.

stir the nuts into the rice just before serving. Serve immediately.

Serves 4–6
Preparation time: *5 minutes*
Cooking time: *25 minutes*

clipboard: Ghee is often used as a cooking fat in Indian cookery. It is clarified butter, the best being from buffalo's milk, which is twice as rich in fat as cow's milk. The advantage of clarified butter, which has had all the milk solids removed, is that it can be heated to a high temperature without burning.

Braised Sweet and Sour Red Cabbage

500 g/1 lb red cabbage, quartered, cored and finely shredded

1 onion, sliced

1 garlic clove, finely chopped

375 g/12 oz cooking apples, peeled, cored and sliced

2 tablespoons demerara sugar

pinch of ground mace

pinch of ground nutmeg

pinch of ground cinnamon

¼ teaspoon ground allspice

¼ teaspoon grated fresh root ginger

2 tablespoons red wine vinegar

150 ml/¼ pint vegetable stock or water

50 g/2 oz butter

salt and pepper

chopped parsley, to garnish

combine the cabbage, onion, garlic, apples, sugar, spices and grated ginger in a large flameproof casserole dish. Season with salt and pepper. Mix the vinegar with the stock or water and pour over the cabbage. Dot with the butter, then cover closely with greaseproof paper and a tight-fitting lid. Bring to the boil, then reduce the heat and simmer for 1½ hours, until the cabbage is tender. Serve garnished with chopped parsley.

alternatively the casserole dish can be transferred to a preheated oven at 160°C/325°F/Gas Mark 3 after the liquid has been brought to the boil. Stir once or twice during the cooking time. This is traditionally served with goose, duck, pheasant and pork.

Serves 6–8
Preparation time: *15 minutes*
Cooking time: *1½ hours*

clipboard: This is an excellent dish to prepare in large quantities, as it both freezes and reheats particularly well. White cabbage can be used instead of red cabbage, but the colour is less inviting.

Wine with Food

Choosing wine

Choosing wine to accompany food is perhaps more difficult than it was just a few years ago. Not only are there many more wines to choose from but the food we eat has also changed, making the old idea that white wine should be served with fish and red with meat irrelevant. It is true that red wine is not really suitable with cod in parsley sauce, but nowadays we are just as likely to be serving seared tuna steaks with a spicy marinade, which would be good with a red wine. The choice of wine will depend entirely on the specific dish, not just whether it is meat, fish or vegetables. Having said this, attitudes are far more relaxed and people are happy to experiment. If you take the following considerations into account your guests will be happy to go along with whatever you choose. Pick a robust wine to accompany robust flavours and a lighter wine for lighter dishes; neither food nor wine should dominate the other. Wine can also complement or contrast with a dish in terms of flavour and texture. A creamy dish could be accompanied by a creamy wine, such as an oaked Chardonnay, or a fresher wine like a Riesling, to add a note of contrast. It is a good idea to think in terms of cooking. A fresh, dry wine will have the same effect as a squeeze of lemon, while a fruity red will add a note of sweetness. Before the meal, why not offer a fortified wine such as sherry or a punch like sangria?

Wine glasses

Most people have a set of general purpose wine glasses, and allow just one per person for informal entertaining. For formal occasions serve different wines in different glasses. Sparkling wines should be served in Champagne flutes to stop the bubbles escaping, red wine in wide, rounded glasses and white wine in tall, narrower ones.

Serving wine

Most white wines and rosés should be served chilled. Reds should be served at room temperature. A good red will benefit from being opened a couple of hours before serving to allow it to breathe. Serving wine at the right temperature will make an average wine taste good and a good wine taste great.

Spinach
with Olive Oil and Lemon Dressing

This simple vegetable dish is traditionally served as an accompaniment to roast lamb, but it is also very good with roast or grilled chicken. It is usually served lukewarm rather than piping hot.

625 g/1¼ lb spinach
2 tablespoons butter
2 garlic cloves, finely chopped
4 tablespoons olive oil
2 tablespoons lemon juice
salt and pepper
shredded lemon rind, to garnish

wash the spinach in a colander and shake off the excess water. Put the spinach in a large saucepan, sprinkling the layers with salt to taste. Cover the pan and cook over a moderate heat for 1–2 minutes until the spinach has wilted and is tender, shaking the pan vigorously from time to time.

drain the spinach thoroughly in a colander, then return it to the pan and toss over a high heat until any remaining water is driven off. Add the butter and garlic and continue tossing until combined with the spinach.

turn the spinach into a serving dish. Drizzle with oil and lemon juice, season with salt and pepper to taste, and garnish with lemon rind.

Serves 6
Preparation time: *about 10 minutes*
Cooking time: *5 minutes*

clipboard: Spinach originally came from Persia but is now grown worldwide. It is available all year round and is highly nutritious, being rich in iron and vitamins.

Grilled Vegetables
with Dipping Sauce

Grilling brings out the true character of food, intensifying its succulence and magnifying its flavour.

4 garlic cloves, finely chopped
10–12 tablespoons extra virgin olive oil
4 baby aubergines, halved lengthways
1 large red onion, sliced into rings
4 baby fennel bulbs
1 large red pepper, cored, deseeded and thickly sliced
1 large yellow pepper, cored, deseeded and thickly sliced
4 baby courgettes, halved lengthways
1 chicory head, halved lengthways
4 large field mushrooms, stems removed
Salsa Verde (see page 144), to serve

Garnish
1 large lemon, cut into wedges
flat-leaf parsley sprigs

put the garlic and olive oil in a bowl and leave to infuse while preparing the vegetables.

score the flesh of the aubergines crisscross-style using the point of a sharp knife. Brush all the vegetables with the garlic-flavoured oil.

cook the vegetables on a baking sheet under a preheated grill, or on a hot ridged griddle pan. Start with the vegetables that take longest, gradually adding the rest until they are all done – onions and fennel take 10–20 minutes; peppers, aubergines and courgettes take 15 minutes; and chicory and mushrooms take 5 minutes. Turn the vegetables during cooking and raise or lower the grill pan as required. When ready, the vegetables should be *al dente*, coloured and blistering.

arrange the vegetables on a large platter or individual plates and garnish with lemon wedges and sprigs of parsley. Offer salsa verde separately, and serve the vegetables warm with crusty bread.

Serves 4
Preparation time: *20 minutes*
Cooking time: *20 minutes*

Honey-Glazed Turnips

Baby turnips are small and tender, with a slightly sweet flavour, and are the perfect vegetable for this interesting treatment.

750 g/1½ lb baby turnips
50 g/2 oz unsalted butter
2 heaped tablespoons clear honey
2 tablespoons toasted flaked or slivered almonds
salt and pepper
1½ tablespoons chopped fresh coriander, to garnish

cook the turnips in salted boiling water for about 10 minutes until tender but still *al dente*. Drain.

melt the butter with the honey in a frying pan. Add the turnips and cook, stirring, for 3–5 minutes until glossy.

stir in the almonds, then pile the turnips into a warm serving dish. Season with salt and pepper to taste. Pour the pan juices over the turnips and garnish with the chopped coriander.

Serves 4–6
Preparation time: *10 minutes*
Cooking time: *10 minutes*

clipboard: Almonds are a versatile ingredient, used in both sweet and savoury dishes, to which they add texture and crunch as well as flavour. Unshelled nuts can be stored in a cool place for up to 6 months, while shelled nuts can be kept in an airtight container in the freezer or refrigerator for up to 6 months.

Carrots
with Ginger and Orange Butter

This is a really simple way of spicing up carrots.

I kg/2 lb carrots, sliced or whole baby carrots
chervil sprigs, to garnish

Ginger and orange butter
50 g/2 oz butter, softened
I teaspoon grated root ginger
½ teaspoon grated orange rind
½ tablespoon orange juice
½ teaspoon clear honey
I tablespoon chopped chervil
salt and pepper

steam or boil the carrots for 10–12 minutes until tender.

meanwhile make the ginger and orange butter. Place all the ingredients in a food processor and blend until smooth and evenly combined.

transfer the cooked carrots to a warm serving dish, add the butter and toss together well until the carrots are thoroughly coated with the butter. Serve immediately, garnished with chervil sprigs.

Serves 4–6
Preparation time: *10 minutes*
Cooking time: *10–15 minutes*

clipboard: Ginger freezes well – simply wrap it in clingfilm or a small freezer bag. Use the amount you want, then return the rest to the freezer for future use. Chervil, which is a pretty herb with feathery fern-like leaves, is used in this recipe for its delicate flavour. The flavour can be destroyed by heat, so it is better to add the chervil after cooking, as in this recipe.

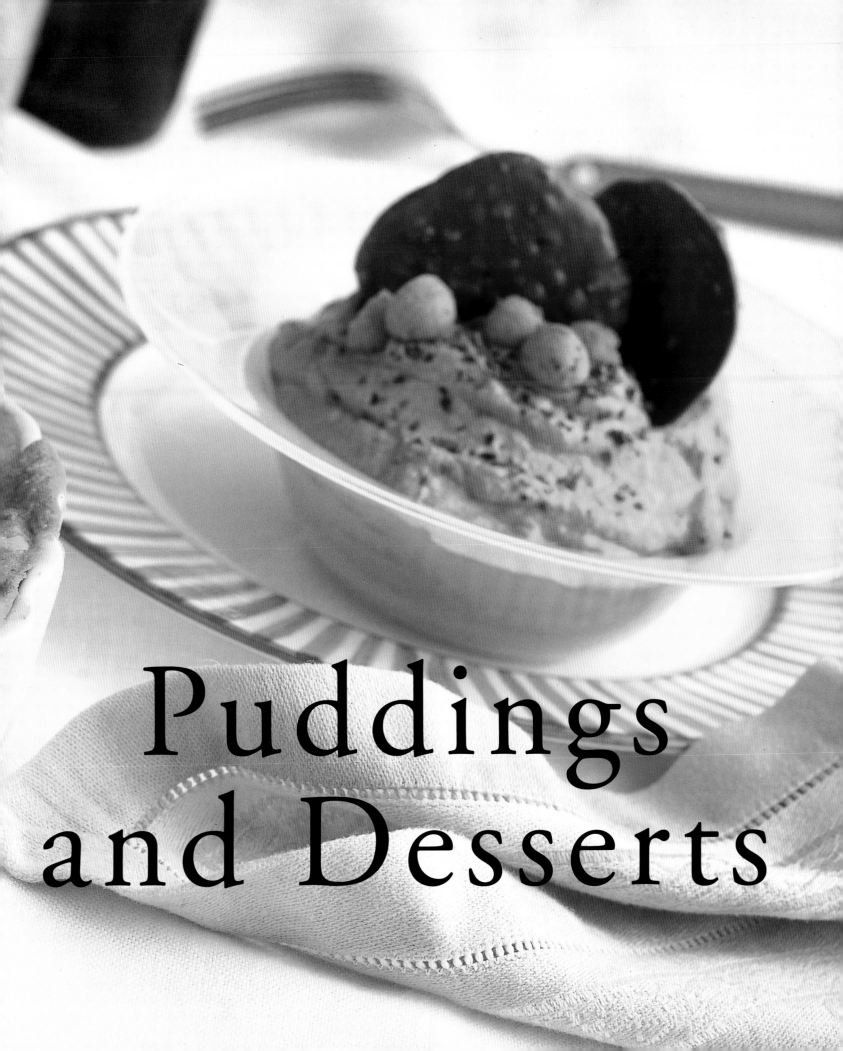

Puddings
and Desserts

Mocha Bombe

250 g/8 oz plain chocolate, chopped

Coffee ice cream
2 tablespoons instant coffee powder
2 tablespoons boiling water
2 egg whites
125 g/4 oz caster sugar
300 ml/10 fl oz double cream

melt the chocolate in a heatproof bowl over a small saucepan of gently simmering water.

put a 1.2 litre/2 pint basin in the freezer to chill for 10 minutes. Pour the chocolate into the basin and rotate to coat the inside completely. Place the basin in a bowl of crushed ice and continue rotating until the chocolate has set in a layer.

to make the ice cream, mix the coffee powder with the water and leave to cool. Whisk the egg whites until stiff, then gradually whisk in the sugar. Whip the cream with the coffee mixture until it forms soft peaks. Fold into the meringue mixture.

spoon into the chocolate mould, smooth the top evenly, cover with foil, remove from the bowl of crushed ice and freeze until firm.

to serve, dip the basin into cold water, invert on to a serving plate and give a sharp shake to turn out.

Serves 6–8
Preparation time: *30 minutes, plus chilling and freezing*

Iced Zabaione

Zabaione is a favourite Italian dessert. It is light and creamy, made with eggs, Marsala and double cream, and decorated with pistachio nuts. This iced version is delicious for summer evenings.

4 egg yolks
75 g/3 oz icing sugar, sifted
4 tablespoons Marsala
125 ml/4 fl oz double cream
chopped pistachio nuts, to decorate

place the egg yolks in a bowl with the icing sugar and whisk until thick and mousse-like.

whip the Marsala and cream together until thick, then carefully fold into the egg mixture.

pour into 4 freezerproof ramekins, cover, seal and freeze. Sprinkle with chopped pistachio nuts to serve.

Serves 4
Preparation time: *20 minutes*

clipboard: Marsala is a Sicilian fortified wine, made in and around the town of the same name. In Italian cooking it is used in savoury as well as sweet dishes.

Lemon Granita

125 g/4 oz sugar
600 ml/1 pint water
thinly pared rind and juice of 3 lemons
4 lemon slices, to decorate

heat the sugar and water gently with the lemon rind over a low heat until the sugar has dissolved, then boil for 5 minutes.

add the lemon juice, cool, then strain.

pour into a rigid freezerproof container, cover, seal and freeze for 2 hours. Whisk and return to the freezer for 2 hours. Whisk again and return to the freezer until firm.

leave at room temperature for 10 minutes just before serving, then stir until crumbly. Spoon into 4 tall glasses. Decorate with lemon slices.

Serves 4
Preparation time: *15 minutes, plus freezing*
Cooking time: *5 minutes*

clipboard: Coffee granita can be made in the same way. Substitute the sugar for 75 g/3 oz soft brown sugar; add 2 tablespoons of coffee granules instead of the lemon juice. To serve, top each dessert with a teaspoon of Tia Maria.

Banana Filo Pie

These delicious baked bananas make a lovely gooey filling for filo pastry.

50 g/2 oz unsalted butter
8 large sheets filo pastry, thawed if frozen
3 firm ripe bananas
25 g/1 oz sultanas
15 g/½ oz soft brown sugar
1 tablespoon dark rum
1 teaspoon grated lemon rind
25 g/1 oz flaked almonds, toasted
icing sugar, to dust

melt 40 g/1½ oz of the butter in a small saucepan. Separate the pastry into sheets. Brush 1 sheet of pastry with the melted butter and top with a second sheet of pastry, brush with butter and repeat twice to give 6 layers of filo pastry. Keep the remaining pastry sheets covered with a damp tea towel to prevent them drying out.

peel and finely slice the bananas and arrange in a 23 cm/9 inch circle in the centre of the pastry. Top the bananas with the sultanas, sugar, rum, lemon rind and almonds and then dot with the remaining butter.

place the remaining 2 sheets of pastry over the top of the pie, brush each sheet of pastry with melted butter and press firmly down around the filling. Using a fluted flan ring or plate, cut around the pie, making sure you leave a 1 cm/½ inch edge.

brush over the remaining melted butter and transfer to a baking sheet. Bake in a preheated oven, 190°C/375°F/Gas Mark 5, for 25–30 minutes. Allow the pie to cool slightly and serve dusted with icing sugar.

Serves 6
Preparation time: *20 minutes*
Cooking time: *30–35 minutes*
Oven temperature: *190°C/375°F/Gas Mark 5*

clipboard: Sometimes spelled phyllo, filo pastry is made from a wheat flour dough which is rolled into tissue-thin sheets. It is common in Greek and Middle Eastern cookery. It is available frozen from most supermarkets, and fresh from a few. Fresh is easier to handle.

Pineapple Pavlova

4 egg whites
250 g/8 oz caster sugar
1 tablespoon cornflour
2 teaspoons vinegar
125 g/4 oz hazelnuts, ground and toasted

Filling
1 small pineapple, finely sliced
3 tablespoons Kirsch
300 ml/10 fl oz double cream
3 kiwi fruit, sliced

whisk the egg whites until stiff. Add the sugar 1 tablespoon at a time, whisking until the meringue is very stiff. Whisk in the cornflour and vinegar, then carefully fold in the hazelnuts.

pile the meringue on to a baking sheet lined with nonstick baking paper. Spread into a 20 cm/8 inch round, hollowing out the centre slightly. Bake in a preheated oven, 150°C/300°F/Gas Mark 2, for 1 hour. Leave to cool, peel off the paper and place on a serving dish.

meanwhile make the filling. Place the pineapple slices in a shallow dish, sprinkle with the Kirsch and leave to macerate for 1 hour.

place the cream in a bowl and add the Kirsch from the pineapple. Whip until stiff, then spoon on to the meringue, spreading to the edges.

arrange some overlapping kiwi fruit slices in a circle around the edge. Lay the pineapple slices inside and finish with some more kiwi fruit in the centre.

Serves 8
Preparation time: *20 minutes, plus macerating*
Cooking time: *1 hour*
Oven temperature: *150°C/300°F/Gas Mark 2*

clipboard: Rich in vitamin C, the kiwi fruit is sweet and juicy with green flesh and small black pips. It can be eaten on its own or used in fruit salads and sorbets. It also makes an attractive garnish or decoration.

Warm Espresso Chocolate Pots

Use a good-quality dark chocolate with a high percentage of cocoa solids – at least 70%.

175 g/6 oz dark chocolate, chopped
250 ml/8 fl oz strong espresso coffee
2 tablespoons whisky
50 g/2 oz sugar
6 egg yolks
50 ml/2 fl oz double cream
grated nutmeg, for sprinkling

place the chocolate in a small pan with the coffee and whisky, and heat gently until the chocolate has melted. Add the sugar and stir until dissolved. Remove from the heat.

beat in the egg yolks immediately until thickened. Pour through a fine sieve into 8 small espresso cups or ramekins. Cool and chill for 4 hours or overnight until set.

whip the cream until it just holds its shape and spoon a little on to each chocolate pot. Sprinkle with nutmeg. Pour a small amount of boiling water into a roasting dish to a depth of about 1 cm/½ inch. Sit the chocolate pots in the boiling water for 1 minute, then remove from the water and serve immediately.

Serves 8
Preparation time: *5 minutes, plus chilling*
Cooking time: *5 minutes*

Apple, Blackberry and Marmalade Crumble

500 g/1 lb Bramley apples, peeled, cored and sliced

1 tablespoon lemon juice

50–75 g/2–3 oz caster sugar

50 ml/2 fl oz water

2 tablespoons marmalade

125 g/4 oz blackberries

Topping

40 g/1½ oz butter

75 g/3 oz plain flour

40 g/1½ oz demerara sugar

put the apples into a saucepan with the lemon juice, caster sugar and water and cook gently for 3–5 minutes, until the apples begin to soften. Stir in the marmalade and blackberries and pour into a 900 ml/1½ pint ovenproof pie dish.

to make the topping, rub the butter into the flour and stir in the sugar. Scatter over the fruit mixture, pressing it down slightly. Place in a preheated oven, 200°C/400°F/Gas Mark 6, for 20–25 minutes, until the crumble topping is golden. Serve hot or cold.

Serves 4–6
Preparation time: *30 minutes*
Cooking time: *20–25 minutes*
Oven temperature: *200°C/400°F/Gas Mark 6*

clipboard: Rhubarb, gooseberries and plums can be used instead of apples, in which case you should omit the blackberries. Jumbo or porridge oats can replace some of the flour: use half plain flour and half oats.

Chocolate Syllabub

125 g/4 oz plain chocolate, broken into pieces
3 tablespoons brandy
300 ml/½ pint double cream, whipped
2 egg whites
grated chocolate, to decorate
dessert biscuits, to serve

place the chocolate and brandy in a small pan and heat very gently until melted. Stir until smooth, then leave to cool.

whisk the cream into the cooled chocolate.

whisk the egg whites until they stand in soft peaks then carefully fold into the chocolate mixture.

spoon into individual glasses or bowls and sprinkle with grated chocolate. Serve immediately with dessert biscuits.

Serves 4–6
Preparation time: *15 minutes*
Cooking time: *5 minutes*

Strawberry Choux Ring

50 g/2 oz butter or margarine
150 ml/¼ pint water
65 g/2½ oz plain flour, sifted
2 eggs, beaten
25 g/1 oz flaked almonds
icing sugar, for sprinkling

Filling
300 ml/½ pint double cream
1 tablespoon caster sugar
375 g/12 oz strawberries, halved

melt the butter or margarine in a large pan, add the water and bring to the boil. Add the flour all at once and beat until the mixture leaves the sides of the pan. Allow to cool slightly, then add the eggs a little at a time, beating vigorously.

spoon the choux paste on to a dampened baking sheet to form a 20 cm/8 inch ring. Sprinkle with the almonds and bake in a preheated oven, 220°C/425°F/Gas Mark 7, for 15 minutes. Lower the heat to 190°C/375°F/Gas Mark 5 and bake for a further 20–25 minutes until golden brown. Set aside to cool on a wire rack.

whip the cream until it holds its shape, then fold in the caster sugar and 250 g/8 oz of the strawberries.

split the ring in half horizontally and pile the filling into the hollow bottom half. Cover with the remaining strawberries then replace the top half of the choux ring. Sprinkle with icing sugar.

Serves 6
Preparation time: *30 minutes*
Cooking time: *35–40 minutes*
Oven temperature: *220°C/425°F/Gas Mark 7*

Exotic Ruby Fruit Salad *with Cardamom*

This beautiful crimson fruit salad is flavoured with cardamom, a fragrant spice often used in Indian, Middle Eastern and North African cooking. The flavour will be enhanced and the fruit will take on an even deeper red if the salad is left to macerate for 2–3 hours before serving.

1.5 kg/3 lb tropical fruits (such as mango, papaya, pineapple, lychee, tamarillo, guava or physalis or other fruit of your choice)
4 green cardamom pods
300 ml/½ pint freshly squeezed ruby red orange juice
I tablespoon orange liqueur, such as Grand Marnier or Cointreau

prepare the fruit according to type. Cut into bite-sized pieces and place in a serving bowl.

split open the cardamom pods, take out the little black seeds and grind them finely with a pestle and mortar. Sprinkle over the fruit.

combine the orange juice and liqueur in a jug, pour over the fruit and stir well to coat.

Serves 4–6
Preparation time: *15 minutes*

clipboard: The cardamom pod is a small, pale green, oval-shaped pod, enclosing some small black seeds. Cardamom is a member of the ginger family. It is a highly aromatic spice and can be used either whole or ground. It adds a delicious spicy flavour to many sweet dishes such as this one.

The Cheeseboard

Choosing cheeses

With a little thought and care, a cheeseboard can be one of the highlights of a meal, particularly if the flavours and textures are well balanced. It is often better to serve cheese before dessert, especially if you are planning to serve a dessert wine as it is difficult to go from a sweet wine back to something drier. Choose a small number of cheeses so the flavour of each is easily identifiable. Texture is as important as flavour when choosing cheese. An ideal cheeseboard would contain one hard cheese, such as a cheddar; one semi-soft cheese, such as a mild, washed-rind cheese; one soft cheese such as a ripe brie or a goats' cheese; and one mild blue cheese. But your choice will also depend on what looks good in the shop and what is ripe enough to eat when you need it.

Presenting cheese

It is worth taking the time to make a cheeseboard look good. Cheeses are attractive in their own right and as they need air to circulate around them, serve any accompaniments separately. Serve the cheese on a flat basket or a wooden or marble board, perhaps decorated with a few figs, grapes or some vine leaves at the most.

Biscuits or bread?

Some people prefer to eat many cheeses on their own, but it is a good idea to offer bread or biscuits for those

who like them. Crusty bread is preferable, with perhaps a few plain crackers and oatcakes as an alternative. Butter is another contentious subject: some people enjoy it and others prefer their cheese without. If you do serve butter, choose an unsalted one to prevent it interfering with the flavours of the cheeses.

Fruit

Fruit is a nice companion to cheese. It offers a fresh, contrasting flavour for those eating cheese, and something to nibble on for those who aren't. Try fresh figs, black or green grapes, apples or pears. Many people also like to serve a few sticks of celery, but this only really goes well with salty, blue cheeses such as Stilton.

Wine

Cheeses vary so much in flavour and intensity, that it is impossible to suggest one type of wine that will go with all of them. The same rules apply as when choosing wine to accompany food: the deeper the flavour of the cheese, the more full-bodied the wine should be. Choose crisp whites for fresh cheeses and mild, soft rind cheeses, and full-bodied reds for bloomy rind cheeses such as camembert and strong goats' cheese. Hard cheeses are best served with soft reds or fruity whites, while the saltiness of blue cheeses is best counteracted with sweeter whites or, of course, with port.

Blueberry Shortcake Tart

475 g/15 oz self-raising flour
175 g/ 6 oz chilled butter, diced
125 g/4 oz caster sugar
1 egg, beaten
milk, for glazing
25 g/1 oz flaked almonds
cream or crème fraîche, to serve

Filling
500 g/1 lb blueberries, defrosted if frozen
2 tablespoons caster sugar

sift the flour into a bowl, add the butter and rub it in until the mixture resembles fine breadcrumbs. Stir in the sugar, add the egg and mix to a firm dough, adding a little cold water, if necessary.

roll out two-thirds of the dough and use to line a greased 23 cm/9 inch flan or tart dish. Spread the blueberries evenly over the pastry and sprinkle with the sugar.

roll out the remaining dough and cut into thin strips. Brush the rim of the tart with water and arrange the strips in a lattice pattern over the top. Brush the strips with a little milk and sprinkle with the almonds.

bake in a preheated oven, 190°C/375°F/Gas Mark 5, for 30–35 minutes, until the pie crust is golden and the blueberries are tender. Serve the tart warm or cold with cream or crème fraîche.

Serves 6–8
Preparation time: *25 minutes*
Cooking time: *30–35 minutes*
Oven temperature: *190°C/375°F/Gas Mark 5*

Celebration
Buffets

Chicken Satay

These tasty little chicken skewers are perfect buffet food.

500 g/1 lb chicken breast, finely sliced into
2.5 cm/1 inch x 5 cm/2 inch slices
bamboo skewers, soaked in water for 30 minutes,
(see page 146)

Marinade
1 tablespoon ground cinnamon
1 tablespoon ground cumin
1 teaspoon pepper
150 ml/¼ pint oil
100 ml/3½ fl oz light soy sauce
2 tablespoons light muscovado sugar

Satay sauce
1 tablespoon oil
2 teaspoons red curry paste
3 tablespoons coconut milk
125 ml/4 fl oz water
3 tablespoons light muscovado sugar
125 g/4 oz peanuts, crushed

Garnish
raw onion, roughly chopped
cucumber chunks

put the chicken slices into a container and add all the ingredients for the marinade. Stir very thoroughly and make sure that all the chicken pieces are coated in the marinade. Leave for a minimum of 4 hours, but preferably overnight, stirring occasionally.

meanwhile make the satay sauce. Heat the oil in a wok, add the curry paste and cook for 30 seconds, then add all the remaining ingredients. Stir well and leave to cook over a low heat for 10–15 minutes, stirring occasionally. Add a little more water if you feel the sauce is becoming too thick. Turn the sauce into a small bowl to serve.

thread the chicken pieces carefully on to the soaked bamboo skewers, leaving a little space at either end. Cook them in batches under a hot grill for about 2 minutes, turning once, until cooked through. Keep the cooked chicken warm while you grill the rest.

garnish with chopped raw onion and chunks of cucumber and serve the chicken skewers with satay sauce for dipping.

Makes approximately 16 skewers
Preparation time: *10–15 minutes,*
  plus marinating
Cooking time: *15–20 minutes*

Pork, Parma Ham and Sage Rolls

50 g/2 oz sultanas

4 tablespoons Marsala

4 pork escalopes

4 slices of Parma ham

16 large sage leaves

125 g/4 oz fontina cheese, cut into wafer-thin slices

olive oil, for shallow-frying

salt and pepper

Salsa verde

2 garlic cloves

25 g/1 oz flat-leaf parsley (leaves only)

15 g/½ oz basil leaves

15 g/½ oz dill

15 g/½ oz mint

15 g/½ oz chives

15 g/½ oz chervil

1 tablespoon rinsed capers

1 tablespoon red wine vinegar

1 teaspoon Dijon mustard

300 ml/½ pint olive oil

mix the sultanas with the Marsala and set aside to macerate for 1 hour. Drain and pat the sultanas dry.

take each pork escalope, place between 2 pieces of baking parchment and pound flat with a mallet or rolling pin. Trim each escalope to an approximate rectangle. Top each escalope with a slice of ham, 4 sage leaves, a quarter of the cheese and a quarter of the sultanas. Season with salt and pepper to taste.

roll up the escalopes from one long side and skewer with cocktail sticks to secure. Heat a little oil in a frying pan and fry the pork rolls for 10 minutes over a moderate heat until browned all over. Remove the pork rolls from the frying pan and then leave to cool to room temperature.

meanwhile make the salsa verde. Put the garlic, herbs and capers in a blender or food processor and blend until the herbs are finely chopped. Add the vinegar and mustard. Blend in the oil through the feeder funnel to form a vibrant green sauce. Season with salt and pepper to taste.

remove and discard the cocktail sticks from the pork rolls and slice each roll into bite-sized pieces. Spear with clean cocktail sticks and serve with the prepared salsa verde.

Serves 8
Preparation time: *20 minutes, plus macerating*
Cooking time: *10 minutes*

Spicy Mushroom and Pepper *Skewers*

If fresh shiitake mushrooms are unavailable, dried shiitake mushrooms can be used instead. These will need to be soaked for 2 hours and drained thoroughly.

30 fresh shiitake mushrooms
2 teaspoons ground coriander
1 garlic clove, crushed
½ teaspoon pepper
½ teaspoon salt
2 tablespoons sunflower oil, plus extra for brushing
2 teaspoons lemon juice
3 orange peppers, cored, deseeded and cut into squares
10 bamboo skewers

remove the tough stalks from the mushrooms and make a cross with a knife in the top of each one.

blend together the coriander, garlic, pepper and salt and stir in the sunflower oil and lemon juice. Spread this mixture all over the mushrooms and pepper squares, cover and leave to marinate for at least 1 hour.

thread the mushrooms and pepper squares alternately on to bamboo skewers, allowing three mushrooms and four pepper squares per skewer.

brush the mushroom and pepper skewers with a little oil and place under a preheated hot grill. Grill for 4–5 minutes, turning once, until the mushrooms and peppers are lightly charred and tender. Serve at once. Satay sauce is a good accompaniment (see page 142).

Makes 10 skewers
Preparation time: *18–20 minutes, plus soaking and marinating*
Cooking time: *4–5 minutes*

clipboard: To prevent the bamboo skewers burning, soak them in cold water for 30 minutes before use.

Mini Chicken Kiev

50 g/2 oz unsalted butter, softened
1 garlic clove, crushed
2 teaspoons lemon juice
1 tablespoon chopped parsley
1 tablespoon chopped tarragon
2 large chicken breast fillets, skinned
4 tablespoons flour, seasoned with salt and pepper
2 eggs, beaten
125 g/4 oz dried breadcrumbs
vegetable oil, for shallow-frying
salt and pepper
lemon wedges, to garnish

cream together the butter, garlic, lemon juice and herbs in a small bowl and season with salt and pepper. Form into 4 small blocks, wrap loosely in foil and freeze for 1 hour.

take each chicken breast and cut in half horizontally to form 4 escalopes. Flatten out each one by placing between two sheets of greaseproof paper and tapping firmly with a rolling pin.

remove the butter from the freezer and place a block in the middle of each escalope. Fold in half and secure with wooden cocktail sticks.

dip each chicken parcel in the seasoned flour, then in the beaten egg and finally in the breadcrumbs to coat thoroughly. Chill for several hours or overnight.

heat a shallow layer of oil in a non-stick frying pan and fry the chicken parcels for 15–20 minutes, turning frequently until well browned on all sides. Serve at once, garnished with lemon wedges.

Makes 4
Preparation time: *25 minutes, plus freezing and chilling*
Cooking time: *15–20 minutes*

Prawn and Rocket Piadina

125 g/4 oz plain flour
½ teaspoon salt
5 g/¼ oz butter, softened
75 ml/3 fl oz warm water
chervil, to garnish

Topping
4 tablespoons extra virgin olive oil, plus extra
for drizzling
2 large garlic cloves, crushed
pinch of crushed chilli flakes
½ teaspoon dried oregano
500 g/1 lb raw tiger prawns, peeled and deveined
175 g/6 oz rocket
pepper

sift the flour and salt into a bowl, make a well in the centre and work in the butter and water to form a soft dough. Knead on a lightly floured surface for 10 minutes. Wrap in clingfilm and leave to rest for 30 minutes.

divide the dough into 12 pieces and roll out each one into a 5 cm/2 inch round.

cover with a clean tea towel while preparing the topping.

heat the oil in a large, heavy-based frying pan and, as soon as it stops foaming, add the garlic, chilli flakes and dried oregano, stir well and immediately add the prawns. Cook for 3–4 minutes until the prawns are cooked. Stir in the rocket and cook until wilted. Add pepper to taste and keep warm.

heat a griddle or heavy-based frying pan until hot. Cook 1 piadina dough base at a time for about 1 minute, flip over and cook the underneath for a further 30 seconds until dotted with brown.

transfer the piadina to warm plates, top with the prawn and rocket mixture, and serve at once, garnished with chervil and drizzled with extra olive oil.

Makes 12
Preparation time: *15–20 minutes, plus resting*
Cooking time: *10 minutes*

Fresh Flowers

Fresh flowers are a vital part of any table setting, adding colour and a touch of luxury to the proceedings. The style of the arrangement and the specific flowers chosen will help to set the mood you want for the occasion.

Size and shape

There are many practical considerations when it comes to planning the size and shape of the display. It has to fit easily on the table, leaving enough room for the food and still allowing guests to see each other, so choose a low arrangement that looks good from all sides. Consider an oblong or oval display if the dining table is rectangular and a round one for a round table. Be creative with your containers. A hollowed-out orange or a savoy cabbage makes a fitting and attractive receptacle for the dinner table. Make holes in the cabbage with a skewer and insert the flower stems into the holes at the last minute before the meal.

Choosing flowers

The flowers should fit in with the general colour scheme of the table setting, perhaps picking out the colours of the napkins or the crockery. Avoid heavily scented flowers as they may distract guests from the delicious smells and flavours of the food. Each flower should be as near perfect as possible, because they will be viewed so close-up.

Candlestick displays

Combining flowers and candles makes great sense in terms of space saving. Either insert a candle into a piece of florists' foam on a saucer and arrange the flowers around it; or use a specially designed foam ring that sits on a candlestick around a narrow candle. Don't forget that flowers are flammable.

Floating flowers

A few choice flower heads floating in a bowl of water make an effective display, especially if you choose an attractive bowl. Add floating candles as a finishing touch.

Individual arrangements

If there is no space in the centre of the table, consider making a tiny flower arrangement for each guest as part of their place setting. Even a single flower in a glass or eggcup looks good.

Goats' Cheese and Tomato Puff Tartlets

Serve these delicious tartlets hot either as a starter or as part of a buffet. Accompany them with a salad of bitter leaves.

250 g/8 oz puff pastry, thawed if frozen
3–4 tablespoons olive oil
250 g/8 oz cherry tomatoes, preferably a mixture of red and yellow, sliced
250 g/8 oz goats' cheese, sliced
2 teaspoons chopped thyme
salt and pepper

roll out the pastry on a lightly floured surface and cut into 7.5 cm/3 inch rounds. Place on a greased baking sheet and brush with oil.

divide half the cherry tomatoes between the pastry rounds, leaving a margin of bare pastry around the edge of each. Arrange the goats' cheese over the top and arrange the remaining tomatoes over that. Season with a little salt and pepper. Sprinkle with the thyme and drizzle 1–2 tablespoons of olive oil over the top.

bake in a preheated oven, 220°C/425°F/Gas Mark 7, for 15–20 minutes until the pastry is risen, crisp and golden brown.

Makes 12–15 tartlets
Preparation time: *15 minutes*
Cooking time: *15–20 minutes*
Oven temperature: *220°C/425°F/Gas Mark 7*

clipboard: Goats' cheeses are made in a range of different shapes and sizes and vary in strength. In the absence of goats' cheese, you can use feta cheese instead.

Marinated Goats' Cheese

The herbs and spices that are added to the oil infuse the goats' cheese as it marinates, giving it a wonderfully delicate flavour.

1 teaspoon fennel seeds
1 teaspoon pink peppercorns
250 g/8 oz goats' cheese, such as Sainte Maure
2 garlic cloves, peeled but left whole
2 small green chillies, bruised
2 sprigs rosemary, bruised
2 bay leaves, bruised
olive oil, to cover
crusty French bread, to serve

put the fennel seeds and peppercorns in a small, heavy-based frying pan and heat gently until they start to pop and release an aroma. Leave to cool completely.

roll the cheese into small balls and place in a bowl or jar. Add the cooled fennel seeds and peppercorns, then add the remaining ingredients with sufficient olive oil to cover.

store in a cool place for at least 3 days, but no longer than 1 week. Serve the cheese balls with a little of the oil and chunks of French bread, or spread on to slices of toasted French bread.

Serves 8
Preparation time: *15 minutes, plus marinating*
Cooking time: *5 minutes*

clipboard: The tiny oval seeds of the fennel plant have a liquorice-like flavour, which goes particularly well with breads, sausages, fish soup and, as here, cheese. Toasting them helps bring out their flavour. To bruise an ingredient – as with these bay leaves – is to partially crush it in order to release its flavour.

Piedmontese Peppers

2 small red peppers, halved, cored and deseeded

2 large ripe plum tomatoes

2 garlic cloves, sliced

2 tablespoons balsamic vinegar

8 tablespoons extra virgin olive oil

8 anchovy fillets

4 large basil leaves

salt and pepper

fresh bread, to serve

place the peppers cut-side up in a small roasting pan.

peel the tomatoes by immersing them in boiling water for 1 minute. Drain and discard the skin. Cut the tomatoes in half and place one half in each pepper, cut-side down.

sprinkle the garlic slices over the tomatoes. Combine the vinegar and oil together and drizzle over the tomato-stuffed peppers. Season well with salt and pepper. Pour 2–3 tablespoons of water into the bottom of the tin.

bake in a preheated oven, 220°C/425°F/Gas Mark 7, for 30 minutes. Remove from the oven and carefully arrange the anchovy fillets and basil leaves over the tomatoes and bake for a further 15–30 minutes until the peppers are very tender. Cool slightly and serve the peppers with the pan juices and bread.

Serves 4
Preparation time: *15 minutes*
Cooking time: *45 minutes–1 hour*
Oven temperature: *220°C/425°F/Gas Mark 7*

clipboard: Basil is a delicious summer herb with an intense aroma. It has a great affinity with tomatoes and red peppers, hence its place in this recipe. It is also the main ingredient in pesto sauce, a popular Italian sauce often served with pasta.

Pear, Chicory and Gorgonzola Bruschetta

2 chicory heads
50 g/2 oz butter
2 large ripe pears, cored and sliced
4 slices of crusty Italian bread, preferably 1 day old
1 garlic clove, peeled but left whole
2 tablespoons walnut oil
175 g/6 oz Gorgonzola cheese, diced
salt and pepper

remove the outer leaves from the chicory and discard. Cut each one lengthways into 4 slices.

melt half the butter in a frying pan and fry the pear slices for 2–3 minutes until lightly browned on both sides. Remove with a slotted spoon and set aside.

add the reserved butter to the pan and fry the chicory for 5 minutes on each side until softened and golden.

meanwhile, cut each slice of bread in half and grill under a preheated grill for 1 minute on each side. Rub each side with the garlic and then drizzle liberally with the walnut oil.

top each bruschetta with the cooked chicory and pear slices, place the diced cheese over the pears and return to the grill for 1–2 minutes until bubbling and golden. Serve at once.

Makes 8
Preparation time: *25 minutes*
Cooking time: *10 minutes*

Mini Pissaladière

This is a classic Provençal tart which can be made with a pizza dough as the base or with a pastry case. The topping, however, is always the same — caramelized onions, anchovies and olives.

4 tablespoons olive oil
1 kg/2 lb onions, finely sliced
2 garlic cloves, crushed
2 teaspoons chopped thyme
1 teaspoon salt
1 teaspoon sugar
6 anchovy fillets, halved lengthways
12 black olives, pitted and halved
3 tablespoons freshly grated Parmesan cheese

Pastry
125 g/4 oz plain flour
¼ teaspoon salt
50 g/2 oz butter, diced
1–2 tablespoons iced water

start by making the pastry. Sift the flour and salt into a bowl and rub in the butter until the mixture resembles fine breadcrumbs. Work in enough iced water to form a soft dough. Knead lightly and chill for 30 minutes.

meanwhile, heat the oil in a heavy-based frying pan and fry the onions, garlic, thyme, salt and sugar for about 25 minutes until the onions are golden and caramelized. Set aside to cool.

divide the pastry into 6 pieces, roll each piece on a lightly floured surface and use to line 6 x 7 cm/3 inch tartlet tins. Prick the bases with a fork and chill for a further 20 minutes.

line each pastry case with greaseproof paper and baking beans and bake blind in a preheated oven, 200°C/400°F/Gas Mark 6, for 15 minutes. Remove the beans and greaseproof paper. Leave the oven on.

divide the onion mixture between the pastry cases, garnish the top of each one with a cross of anchovies and four olive pieces. Sprinkle with Parmesan, return to the oven and bake for 10 minutes. Cool on a wire rack and serve warm.

Serves 6
Preparation time: *20 minutes, plus chilling*
Cooking time: *50 minutes*
Oven temperature: *200°C/400°F/Gas Mark 6*

Tabbouleh and Fennel Salad

Fennel adds crunch to this moist bulgar wheat salad.

250 g/8 oz bulgar wheat
I fennel bulb, very finely sliced
I red onion, finely sliced
5 tablespoons chopped mint
5 tablespoons chopped parsley
2 tablespoons fennel seeds, crushed
2 tablespoons olive oil
finely grated rind and juice of 2 lemons
salt and pepper

place the bulgar wheat in a bowl, add enough cold water to cover, then set aside for 30 minutes, until all the water has been absorbed. Line a colander with muslin or a clean tea towel. Drain the bulgar wheat into the colander, then gather up the sides of the cloth or tea towel and squeeze to extract as much of the liquid as possible from the bulgar wheat. Tip the wheat into a salad bowl.

stir in the fennel, onion, mint, parsley, fennel seeds, oil, lemon rind and half the lemon juice. Season with salt and pepper to taste. Cover and set aside for 30 minutes to allow the flavours to develop, then taste the salad and add more lemon juice, if required.

Serves 6
Preparation time: *35 minutes, plus soaking and standing*

clipboard: Bulgar wheat is made by cooking the wheat and then drying and cracking it. It is rich in both protein and carbohydrate. To make a couscous and celery salad, substitute 250 g/8 oz quick-cooking couscous for the bulgar wheat and 6 celery sticks, finely sliced, for the fennel. Proceed as in the main recipe.

Potato and Radish Salad *with vinaigrette*

500 g/1 lb small new potatoes
4 spring onions, sliced
1 bunch of radishes, finely sliced
salt and pepper

Vinaigrette
1 tablespoon white wine vinegar
3 tablespoons extra virgin olive oil
½ teaspoon mustard powder or prepared mustard

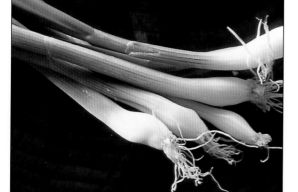

scrub the potatoes clean but leave the skins on. Cook in salted boiling water for about 20 minutes, until tender.

make the vinaigrette by putting all the ingredients in a screw-top jar and shaking vigorously until they are well mixed. Season with salt and pepper to taste.

drain the potatoes well and mix with the vinaigrette while still warm. Set aside to cool.

add the spring onions and radishes, mix well and transfer to a salad bowl to serve.

Serves 4
Preparation time: *10 minutes*
Cooking time: *about 20 minutes*

Orange and Olive Salad

The oranges that work best for this salad have a sharp flavour, not a sweet taste. The olives should be large and fleshy.

2 teaspoons cumin seeds
4 large oranges
125 g/4 oz green olives, pitted and halved
50 ml/2 fl oz olive oil
1 tablespoon harissa (optional)
1 crisp lettuce, torn into bite-sized pieces
salt
sprigs of dill, to garnish

heat a small heavy-based frying pan, add the cumin seeds and dry-fry until fragrant. Tip into a grinder and grind to a powder.

remove the rind from 1 of the oranges with a zester and set aside. Peel the oranges with a sharp knife, carefully removing all the pith. Working over a bowl to catch the juice, cut out the segments from the oranges and discard any pips. Put the oranges and olives into a bowl with the juice.

whisk or shake together the oil, harissa, if using, and roasted cumin. Add salt to taste, then pour the dressing over the oranges and olives and toss together.

arrange the lettuce leaves in a serving dish. Add the orange and olive mixture. Garnish with the reserved orange rind and sprigs of dill and serve.

Serves 4
Preparation time: *10–15 minutes*
Cooking time: *5 minutes*

clipboard: Harissa is a fiery sauce made of red peppers, red chillies, garlic and spices. It gives this salad an extra kick, however, if unavailable, substitute a few drops of Tabasco sauce.

Brown Rice and Vegetable Pilaf

2 tablespoons extra virgin olive oil

1 onion, chopped

2 garlic cloves, chopped

1 teaspoon roasted coriander seeds, crushed

1 teaspoon roasted cumin seeds, crushed

2 dried red chillies, crushed

1 teaspoon ground cinnamon

2 large carrots, sliced

2 celery sticks, sliced

375 g/12 oz brown rice

900 ml/1½ pints vegetable stock

125 g/4 oz French beans, halved

50 g/2 oz green peas, thawed if frozen

50 g/2 oz dried figs, chopped

50 g/2 oz cashew nuts, toasted

2 tablespoons chopped fresh coriander or flat-leaf parsley

salt and pepper

heat the olive oil in a large saucepan, add the onion, garlic and spices and fry gently for 5 minutes. Add the carrots and celery and fry for a further 5 minutes. Season with salt and pepper to taste.

add the rice, stir-fry for 1 minute and then pour in the stock. Bring to the boil, cover and simmer over a gentle heat for 20 minutes. Add all the remaining ingredients and cook for a further 10–15 minutes until the rice is cooked and the vegetables are tender.

Serves 4–6
Preparation time: *25 minutes*
Cooking time: *40–45 minutes*

clipboard: Cashews are the seeds of a tropical fruit called the cashew apple, or pear cashew. Cashew nuts have a rich buttery flavour, which can enhance many sweet and savoury dishes. They do not keep terribly well so if you intend to keep them for longer than a month, they are best stored in the refrigerator or frozen.

Tomato and Coriander Salad

1 kg/2 lb mixed tomatoes, sliced or quartered
(including yellow cherry tomatoes)
2 teaspoons grated lime rind
½ small red onion, finely sliced
1 tablespoon sesame seeds, toasted (optional)
coriander sprigs, to garnish

Dressing
2 tablespoons chopped fresh coriander
1 tablespoon lime juice
1 garlic clove, crushed
½ teaspoon clear honey
pinch of cayenne pepper
4 tablespoons extra virgin olive oil
salt and pepper

start by making the dressing. Whisk together the coriander, lime juice, garlic, honey and cayenne. Season with salt and pepper to taste, then whisk in the oil.

arrange the tomatoes in a large serving bowl and scatter with the lime rind, onion and toasted sesame seeds, if using.

whisk the dressing ingredients once more and pour them over the salad. Cover and set aside for 30 minutes to allow the flavours to develop, before serving. Garnish with coriander sprigs to serve.

Serves 4
Preparation time: *5 minutes, plus marinating*

clipboard: Honey is an excellent addition to salad dressings. Its sweetness cuts across the sour tartness of vinegar, lemon or lime juice.

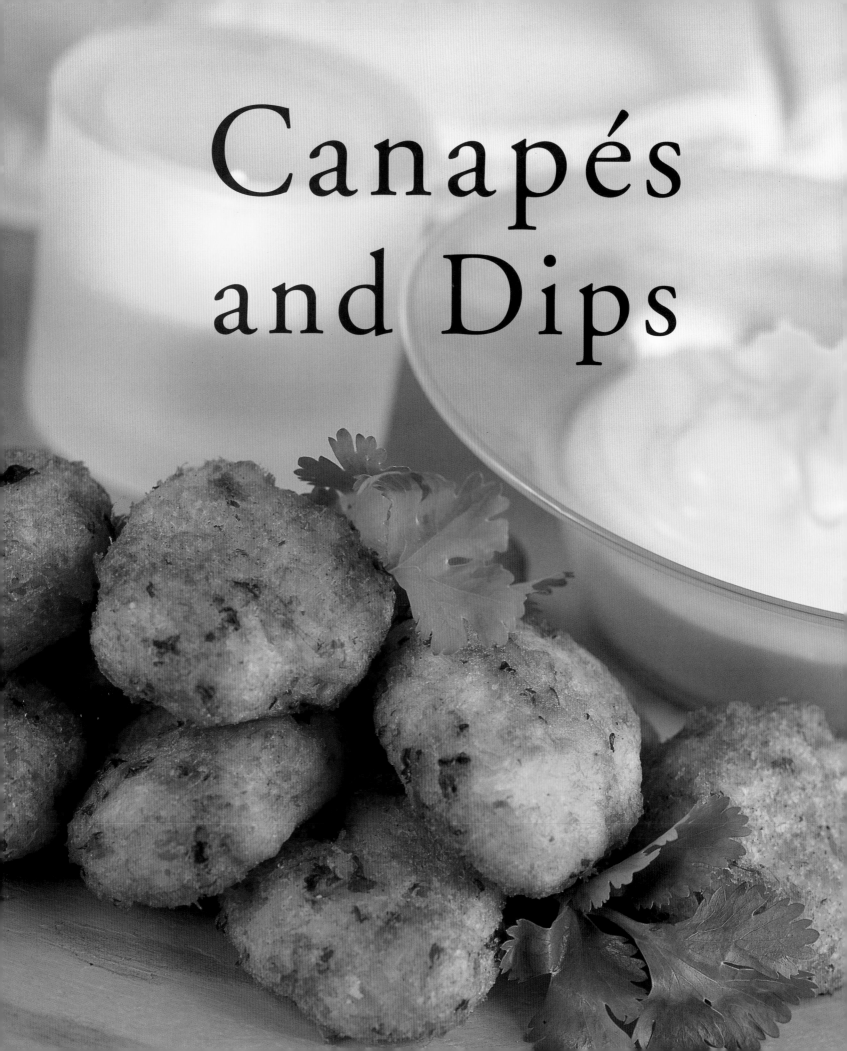

Canapés and Dips

Guacamole

2 large ripe avocados

3 tablespoons lemon or lime juice

2 garlic cloves, crushed

40 g/1½ oz chopped spring onions

1–2 tablespoons chopped mild green chillies

2 tablespoons chopped fresh coriander

125 g/4 oz tomatoes, skinned, seeded and chopped

salt and pepper

tortilla chips, to serve

cut the avocados in half and remove the stones. Scoop out the flesh and sprinkle with a little of the lemon or lime juice to prevent it discolouring.

put the avocado flesh into a bowl with the remaining lemon or lime juice and mash coarsely. Add the garlic, spring onions, chillies and coriander, and season to taste with salt and pepper. Mix in the chopped tomatoes.

cover and chill in the refrigerator for 1 hour. Serve with tortilla chips.

Serves 6
Preparation time: *15 minutes, plus chilling*

clipboard: If you prefer your guacamole smooth, make it in a liquidizer rather than mashing it coarsely, as here. Either way, cover the guacamole tightly with clingfilm to prevent it discolouring in the refrigerator, and do not chill it for more than 1 hour, as any longer may cause it to lose its pretty colour.

Potato Skins
with Soured Cream

5 large baking potatoes, scrubbed and dried
150 ml/¼ pint soured cream
1 teaspoon snipped chives
salt and pepper
vegetable oil, for frying

prick the potatoes with a fork and bake in a preheated oven, 190°C/375°F/Gas Mark 5, for about 1¼ hours until tender. Meanwhile prepare the dip. Mix the soured cream with the chives and salt and pepper to taste. Spoon into a bowl, cover and chill.

leave the potatoes to cool for a few minutes, then cut each one in half lengthways then again to make 4 long pieces. Using a teaspoon scoop out most of the potato, leaving just a thin layer next to the skin. (Use the removed potato as a topping for a vegetable pie.)

pour the vegetable oil into a pan to a depth of 7 cm/3 inches. Heat the oil to 190°C/375°F or until a cube of bread browns in 30 seconds. Fry 4–5 potato skins at a time for about 2 minutes until brown and crisp. Remove from the oil with a slotted spoon and drain on kitchen paper. Keep the cooked skins hot in the oven while you cook the remaining skins. Sprinkle lightly with salt and serve with the soured cream dip.

Makes 20
Preparation time: *15 minutes, plus chilling*
Cooking time: *1½–1¾ hours*
Oven temperature: *190°C/375°F/Gas Mark 5*

Monkfish Bites
with Mint Dip

4 tablespoons lemon juice
4 tablespoons oil
2 teaspoons white wine vinegar
1 onion, finely chopped
1 tablespoon chopped mint
1 kg/2 lb monkfish
salt and pepper

Mint dip
3 tablespoons thick mayonnaise
3 tablespoons thick natural yogurt
1 teaspoon lemon juice
2 tablespoons chopped mint
½ tablespoon caster sugar
mint sprigs, to garnish

combine the lemon juice, oil, vinegar, onion and mint in a bowl, and season to taste.

cut the monkfish into 2.5 cm/1 inch cubes, making sure all the skin and bones are removed. Add the fish to the marinade, cover and leave to stand in a cool place for 2 hours.

make the mint dip by mixing together all the ingredients and season with salt and pepper to taste. Spoon the dip into a small bowl, cover with clingfilm and chill in the refrigerator.

drain the pieces of fish and thread them on to long skewers. Cook under a preheated moderate grill for about 5 minutes on each side until cooked through. Serve garnished with mint, accompanied by the mint dip.

Serves 20, as part of a buffet
Preparation time: *25 minutes, plus marinating*
Cooking time: *about 10 minutes*

clipboard: Try to serve the monkfish bites as freshly cooked as possible. Ideally, they should be grilled about 30 minutes before serving.

Spicy Palmiers

This recipe makes a tasty pre-dinner snack and, if you use frozen pastry, it is very quick to prepare.

250 g/8 oz puff pastry, thawed if frozen
2 tablespoons olive oil
½ teaspoon paprika
pinch of ground cayenne
3 teaspoons freshly grated Parmesan cheese

roll out the puff pastry thinly on a lightly floured surface and trim to make a 20 x 25 cm/8 x 10 inch rectangle.

combine the oil, paprika, cayenne and Parmesan and brush three-quarters of the paste all over the pastry to give an even coating.

fold in both long sides of pastry to meet in the middle, spread on the remaining paste and fold the pastry in half lengthways. Press down firmly.

cut into 24 thin slices using a sharp knife and transfer, cut side down, to 2 greased baking sheets.

bake in a preheated oven, 200°C/400°F/Gas Mark 6, for 10 minutes, then turn over and bake for a further 4–5 minutes until the pastries are crisp and golden. Set aside to cool on a wire rack. These are best eaten the same day.

Makes 24
Preparation time: *10 minutes*
Cooking time: *15 minutes*
Oven temperature: *200°C/400°F/Gas Mark 6*

clipboard: Paprika is made from mild varieties of capsicum, or sweet pepper, which have had their seeds and inner membranes removed before being dried and ground. It should be bought in small quantities and replaced often as both flavour and colour deteriorate rapidly. It should be a bright red colour, which shows that it is fresh.

Table Setting

A beautifully laid table will instantly transform a meal into a special occasion, making your guests feel welcome, relaxed and pampered. It is important to set the right mood for the occasion, whether it is an informal summer lunch party, Christmas dinner, or a dinner party for business colleagues. For the best effect, choose a theme or at least a colour scheme to work to, then choose your table cloth, napkins, crockery, serving dishes and flowers accordingly. In spring or summer, use either whites and pale pastels, or vibrant pinks, lime greens and bright oranges cooled down with the addition of whites. In autumn or winter, choose more subdued tones to set the scene, perhaps terracotta, steel grey and blue, or deep purples and pinks. Rich reds and greens are generally associated with Christmas meals, but why not try white and gold or royal blue instead to make a change? The table cloth will have the strongest effect on the scheme, so take care with strongly-coloured or patterned cloths unless you want to make a bold statement and you have chosen the other elements carefully. Napkins also provide points of colour and can be folded into mitres or other spectacular shapes for special meals, or could be simply decorated with fresh flowers. Alternatively, use co-ordinating napkin rings in silver, wood, papier mâché or ceramic. Whatever the occasion, the times you are entertaining are probably your only opportunities for using your best cutlery, glasses and crockery, so it seems a shame not to use them however informal the occasion, and you will certainly flatter your friends or relatives. Remember to choose serving dishes which will enhance the scheme, rather than detract from it. Make sure the china, glasses and cutlery are sparklingly clean or the effect will be lost. Try to incorporate candles into your table settings for evening meals as they cast a wonderfully soft light which provides instant atmosphere in any room.

Olives *Marinated with Asian Flavours*

250 g/8 oz mixed green and black olives
1 garlic clove, crushed
1 teaspoon grated ginger
2 lime leaves, shredded, or grated rind of 1 lime
2 red chillies, bruised
2 tablespoons dark soy sauce
4 tablespoons extra virgin olive oil

place the olives in a bowl, add the remaining ingredients and stir well. Cover and refrigerate for up to 1 week.

Serves 8
Preparation time: *5 minutes*

clipboard: For a variation of the above recipe, combine the following ingredients in a small bowl: 250 g/8 oz large green olives, 2 sliced garlic cloves, the grated rind of ½ a lemon, 1 tablespoon balsamic vinegar, ½ teaspoon chilli flakes and 4 tablespoons extra virgin olive oil. Cover and keep in the refrigerator for up to 3 days.

Lamb and Mint Meatballs

500 g/1 lb minced lamb
2 garlic cloves, crushed
2 teaspoons mint sauce
1 egg, beaten
oil, for shallow-frying
salt and pepper
mint leaves, to garnish

Piquant dip
50 g/2 oz demerara sugar
2 teaspoons cornflour
3 tablespoons water
4 tablespoons redcurrant jelly
2 tablespoons Worcestershire sauce

put the lamb in a bowl and add the garlic and mint sauce. Season well with salt and pepper and bind the mixture with the egg. With floured hands, roll into walnut-sized balls.

heat the oil in a frying pan, add the meatballs in batches and fry for about 10 minutes until they are golden brown. Drain on kitchen paper and keep warm.

to make the dip, put the sugar, cornflour and water in a small pan and blend in the redcurrant jelly and Worcestershire sauce. Bring slowly to the boil and cook, stirring, until smooth.

spear the meatballs and mint leaves on cocktail sticks and serve warm, with the dip.

Makes about 25
Preparation time: *10 minutes*
Cooking time: *15–20 minutes*

clipboard: Mint blends especially well with lamb. It has a cool, fresh character, which is the perfect accompaniment.

Salt Cod Fritters

250 g/8 oz salt cod
150 ml/¼ pint milk
250 g/8 oz potatoes, peeled and cubed
1 garlic clove, crushed
2 spring onions, finely chopped
1 tablespoon chopped fresh coriander
1 egg yolk
oil, for shallow-frying
pepper

To garnish
shredded lemon rind
fresh coriander sprigs
mayonnaise, to serve

put the salt cod into a bowl and cover with cold water. Leave to soak for 24 hours, changing the water several times.

drain the fish and dry well. Remove the skin and bones and cut the flesh into small cubes. Place in a bowl, cover with the milk and leave for 2 hours.

drain the cod and place in a pan with the potatoes. Cover with water, bring to the boil and simmer, covered, for 20 minutes until the cod and potatoes are tender.

drain and mash the fish and potatoes together. Beat in the remaining ingredients except for the oil, and season with pepper.

heat about 2.5 cm/1 inch of oil in a deep frying pan. Drop teaspoons of the cod mixture into the oil. Fry for 1–2 minutes until the fritters are browned on all sides.

drain on kitchen paper and keep warm while frying the remaining fritters. Garnish with lemon rind and coriander and serve hot with mayonnaise.

Serves 8
Preparation time: *35 minutes, plus soaking*
Cooking time: *30 minutes*

Falafel

These savoury patties are a traditional Middle Eastern snack. The mixture is quite wet and crumbly when you come to shape it, but this ensures a perfect, light texture once the patties are fried.

125 g/4 oz frozen broad beans, defrosted
2 tablespoons Greek yogurt
1 tablespoon tahini paste
1 tablespoon lemon juice
1 garlic clove, crushed
1 teaspoon ground coriander
½ teaspoon ground cumin
½ teaspoon cayenne pepper
1 tablespoon chopped fresh coriander
1 tablespoon chopped mint
oil for shallow-frying
salt and pepper
Greek yogurt with shredded mint leaves, to serve

drain the broad beans and dry thoroughly. Place in a food processor and blend to form a fairly smooth paste. Transfer the puréed beans to a bowl. Stir in all the remaining ingredients, except the oil, and season with salt and pepper. Cover and chill for 1 hour.

form the mixture into small patties. Heat a shallow layer of oil in a frying pan and fry the patties, a few at a time, for 1–2 minutes on each side until golden brown.

drain on kitchen paper and keep warm while frying the remaining falafel. Serve hot with Greek yogurt flavoured with mint.

Makes approximately 12
Preparation time: *10 minutes, plus chilling*
Cooking time: *6–8 minutes*

clipboard: Tahini is an oily paste made of ground, raw sesame seeds. It is often used in Middle Eastern cooking.

Avocado Salsa

1 firm, ripe avocado
2 tablespoons lime juice
1 tablespoon finely chopped coriander
2 spring onions, finely sliced
salt and pepper
diced red pepper, to garnish

cut lengthways through the centre of the avocado as far as the stone, then gently twist the two halves apart. Remove the stone, peel off the skin and cut the avocado into 1 cm/½ inch dice.

put the avocado flesh into a bowl with the lime juice, coriander and spring onions. Season to taste with salt and pepper and toss lightly to combine without damaging the avocado. Cover and refrigerate until required. Serve garnished with diced red pepper.

Serves 4
Preparation time: *10 minutes*

clipboard: This salsa makes a great accompaniment to warm dishes, such as Falafel (see page 192), Lamb and Mint Meatballs (see page 189) and Chicken Satay (see page 142), especially as part of a buffet.

Cocktails

Classic Champagne Cocktail

1 sugar lump
1 orange
2–3 drops of Angostura bitters
½ teaspoon Cognac
½ teaspoon Triple Sec or apricot brandy
100 ml/3½ fl oz Champagne, chilled

rub the sugar lump over the skin of the orange, then place in a champagne flute. Drop the bitters on to the sugar lump, then add the Cognac and Triple Sec or apricot brandy. Leave for as long as possible – at least 45 minutes – for the flavours to blend. To serve, pour in the Champagne and serve at once.

Makes 1
Preparation time: *10 minutes, plus resting*

Bloody Mary

If you do not have any Tabasco sauce, add a pinch of cayenne pepper or celery salt to your Bloody Mary.

25 ml/1 fl oz vodka
125 ml/4 fl oz tomato juice
2 dashes of Worcestershire sauce
1 teaspoon lemon juice
a dash of Tabasco sauce
salt and pepper

To decorate
1 lemon slice
1 mint sprig or celery stick

shake all the ingredients together with ice and strain into a tumbler or balloon wine glass. Add salt and pepper to taste. Decorate with a sprig of mint or a celery stick.

Makes 1
Preparation time: *5 minutes*

clipboard: Bloody Maria is a version made with tequila instead of vodka. Virgin Mary omits the vodka.

Serving Cocktails

Cocktails are always popular, whether it is one or two served as an aperitif before a meal or many more served at a cocktail party. All you really need to serve cocktails are a few simple glasses and a cocktail shaker or electric blender for mixing. Basic wine glasses are suitable for most, but if you have a wider selection of glasses, choose tumblers for drinks served over ice; tall, straight glasses for high-balls; and Champagne flutes for sparkling drinks as they are specially designed to stop the bubbles escaping. Part of the fun of serving cocktails is the decoration. Some cocktails have traditional decorations, such as an olive served with a dry

martini or tequila-based drinks served in salt-rimmed glasses. With other drinks you can use your imagination. Decorations can be divided into three categories: those served on the edge of the glass, such as a slice of lemon; those speared on cocktail sticks, such as cherries or olives; and those floated in the drink, such as mint leaves. Choose from herb sprigs, fruit slices, olives, Maraschino cherries, whole strawberries or raspberries, cinnamon sticks, citrus rind spirals, grated nutmeg, celery sticks, sliced banana, apple, cucumber or pineapple, or pared citrus rind, selecting the decoration to relate to the

cocktail. Make the decorations in advance so they are ready when you need them. For a special occasion, buy brightly coloured straws, paper parasols and cocktail swizzle sticks to add to the fun. When planning a cocktail party, remember to make lots of ice in advance; you always need more than you think you will. It is also a good idea to have more than one corkscrew at the ready as they are easy to mislay. If you are serving cocktails before a meal, offer guests at least a few nuts or olives to accompany them. For a full-scale cocktail party, serve more substantial finger food (see the Canapés and Dips chapter for ideas).

Margarita

The Margarita cocktail is a sophisticated way of enjoying tequila.

40 ml/1½ fl oz tequila
25 ml/1 fl oz fresh lime juice
15 ml/½ fl oz Triple Sec

shake the ingredients thoroughly with ice and strain into a salt-rimmed cocktail glass.

Serves 1
Preparation time: *5 minutes*

clipboard: To coat a glass rim with salt, rub it first with a piece of lime, then dip it into a pile of salt which will stick to the moist rim.

Mulled Red Wine

8–9 bottles red wine
375 g/12 oz raisins
500 g/1 lb caster sugar
4 cinnamon sticks
finely pared rind of 1 lemon
finely pared rind of 1 orange
20 whole cloves
2.5 litres/4 pints boiling water
450 ml/¾ pint brandy
2 lemons, thinly sliced
2 oranges, thinly sliced

put the wine into a large saucepan or preserving pan. Add the raisins, sugar, cinnamon sticks, lemon and orange rinds and cloves.

bring to the boil slowly, stirring continuously until all the sugar has dissolved. Simmer very gently for 20–25 minutes, stirring occasionally. Add the water and brandy and barely bring back to the boil. Add the slices of lemon and orange. At this stage, the mixture may be allowed to cool and can be reheated when you are ready to serve.

ladle into glasses, putting a spoon into each one before you pour in the wine. (Pouring the hot liquid over a spoon prevents glasses from cracking or breaking.)

Makes about 60 glasses
Preparation time: *10–15 minutes*
Cooking time: *about 30 minutes*

clipboard: The boxes of wine available from most supermarkets and off licences are suitable for mulling. Use the least expensive brandy you can find.

Tom Collins

ice cubes
juice of ½ lemon
1½ teaspoons caster sugar
60 ml/2 fl oz gin
soda water, to top up

To decorate
1 lemon slice (optional)
1 maraschino cherry (optional)

half-fill a cocktail shaker or screw-top jar with ice. Add the lemon juice, and stir in the caster sugar. Pour in the gin and shake well for 60 seconds. Strain into a tall tumbler, add more ice and top up with the soda water.

decorate with a slice of lemon and a cherry, if liked.

Serves 1
Preparation time: *5 minutes*

Claret Cup

75 ml/3 fl oz white rum

I miniature bottle of orange-flavoured liqueur

finely pared rind of I lemon

2 bottles claret or other red wine

3 bottles of ginger ale

ice cubes

mint sprigs, to decorate

put the white rum and orange-flavoured liqueur into a small jug. Add the lemon rind, cover and leave to stand for about 2 hours to allow the flavours to develop.

pour the claret and ginger ale into a large bowl, add the rum and orange-flavoured liqueur mixture, with the lemon rind, and stir to mix.

add a handful of ice cubes and serve immediately, decorated with mint.

Serves 12
Preparation time: *10 minutes, plus standing*

clipboard: Orange-flavoured liqueurs include Cointreau, Curaçao, Grand Marnier and Triple Sec.

Prohibition Punch

125 ml/4 fl oz sugar syrup (see below)
350 ml/12 fl oz lemon juice
900 ml/1½ pints apple juice
ice cubes
2.5 litres/4 pints ginger ale

To decorate
orange slices
lemon slices

freeze a large block of ice in a shallow container and break it up into pieces. Mix the sugar syrup and juices together in a large, chilled punch bowl. Add the ice and pour over the ginger ale. Decorate with orange and lemon slices.

Serves 25–30
Preparation time: *10 minutes, plus freezing*

clipboard: To make sugar syrup, put equal quantities of sugar and water into a small pan and bring slowly to the boil, stirring to dissolve the sugar. Boil the mixture for 1–2 minutes without stirring. Allow to cool.

Lemonale

2 litres/3½ pints strong tea, cooled
juice of 6 lemons
6 tablespoons sugar
1 litre/1¾ pints ginger ale

To decorate
mint sprigs
lemon or lime slices

freeze a large block of ice in a shallow container and break it into pieces. Pour the tea into a large bowl or jug. Add the lemon juice, sugar and ice. Stir until the sugar has dissolved. Just before serving, pour in the ginger ale and decorate with mint and lemon or lime.

Serves 20
Preparation time: *10 minutes, plus freezing*

Frosty Lime

1 scoop lime sorbet
4 teaspoons grapefruit juice
4 teaspoons mint syrup (see below)

To decorate
mint sprig
lemon or lime slice

place the sorbet, grapefruit juice and mint syrup into a liquidizer and blend at high speed for about 30 seconds. Strain into a champagne flute or cocktail glass and decorate with the mint sprig. Cut a small slit in the lemon or lime slice and fix on to the rim of the glass.

Makes 1
Preparation time: *5 minutes*

clipboard: To make mint syrup, dissolve 750 g/1½ lb sugar in 250 ml/8 fl oz of water in a small pan over a moderate heat. Add a handful of crushed mint leaves, bring to the boil and boil for 5 minutes. Allow to cool, then strain into a jug.

Iced Apple Tea

25 g/1 oz tea leaves or 1 tea bag
450 ml/¾ pint cold water
450 ml/¾ pint apple juice
juice of 1 lemon
1 teaspoon sugar (optional)
ice cubes

To decorate
8 lemon or orange slices
8 mint sprigs

put the tea and the water in a large jug, leave to steep overnight and strain, if necessary.

add the apple juice, lemon and sugar to taste. Add plenty of ice and garnish with the lemon or orange slices and sprigs of mint. Pour into tall tumblers or tea glasses and serve.

Serves 6–8
Preparation time: *10 minutes, plus steeping*

Roman Punch

1 kg/2 lb caster sugar
juice of 3 oranges
juice of 10 lemons
1.2 litres/2 pints Champagne or sparkling wine
1.2 litres/2 pints dark rum
15 ml/½ fl oz orange bitters
grated rind of 1 orange
10 egg whites, beaten
orange slices, to decorate

put the sugar into a large, chilled punch bowl and pour in the orange and lemon juices. Stir gently until the sugar has dissolved.

add the Champagne or sparkling wine, rum, orange bitters, orange rind and egg whites. Add plenty of ice cubes and stir well. Keep the bowl packed with ice so that the punch remains chilled.

decorate with orange slices before serving.

Serves 15–20
Preparation time: *10 minutes*

Caribbean Champagne

8 ml/¼ fl oz light rum
8 ml/¼ fl oz crème de banane
dash of Angostura bitters
chilled Champagne or sparkling dry
white wine, to top up

To decorate
1 banana slice
1 pineapple slice
1 Maraschino cherry

pour the light rum, crème de banane and Angostura bitters into a Champagne glass.

top up with Champagne or sparkling white wine and stir gently.

decorate with a slice of banana, pineapple and a cherry, all speared on a cocktail stick.

Makes 1
Preparation time: *10 minutes*

Picnics

Spanakopita

1 kg/2 lb fresh spinach
2 tablespoons olive oil
1 onion, chopped
1 teaspoon dried oregano
250 g/8 oz feta cheese, crumbled
4 eggs, beaten
375 g/12 oz filo pastry, thawed if frozen
50 g/2 oz butter, melted
salt, pepper and grated nutmeg

wash the spinach in several changes of water, then place in a large saucepan with only the water that is clinging to the leaves. Cover and cook for 1–2 minutes, shaking the pan occasionally, until the spinach is tender. Drain well, pressing out as much water as possible, then chop the spinach finely and place in a large bowl.

heat the oil in a clean saucepan, add the chopped onion and fry for about 5 minutes until softened. Add to the spinach. Add the oregano and feta, then stir in the eggs with nutmeg, salt and pepper to taste. Mix well.

butter a shallow ovenproof dish, about 25 x 18 cm/10 x 7 inches in size. Layer the filo pastry in the dish, brushing each layer with butter and turning each successive sheet slightly to make angles all round. Continue until you have 3 sheets left.

fill the pie with the spinach mixture. Fold over the edges of the filo pastry to cover the filling. Cover with the remaining filo sheets, tucking them in to fit the top of the dish, and brushing them with melted butter. Bake in a preheated oven, 190°C/375°F/Gas Mark 5, for 45–50 minutes, until the pastry is crisp and golden brown. Serve hot or cold.

Serves 6
Preparation time: *30 minutes*
Cooking time: *45–50 minutes*
Oven temperature: *190°C/375°F/Gas Mark 5*

clipboard: The nutmeg tree originally grew in the Molucca Islands, where it formed a valuable part of the spice trade. The seed of the tree grows within a lacy cage of mace and is dried in the sun after harvesting. It is best bought whole as the powdered variety soon loses its fragrance. It is particularly good with both spinach and cheese, hence its role here.

Picnic Chicken Loaf

This stuffed bread is weighted down overnight, which enables it to be cut into wedges to serve. You will need a round sesame loaf approximately 30 cm/12 inches in diameter.

4 skinless chicken breast fillets
4 skinless, boneless chicken thighs
1 tablespoon lemon juice
½ tablespoon ground turmeric
2 tablespoons olive oil
75 ml/3 fl oz water
3 tablespoons chopped herbs
50 g/2 oz pistachio nuts, toasted and roughly chopped
1 Eastern-style sesame loaf
250 g/8 oz chicken liver pâté
salt and pepper

wash and dry the chicken and rub all over with lemon juice, turmeric and half the oil. Season with salt and pepper. Leave to marinate for 1 hour.

heat the remaining oil in a large, heavy-based frying pan and fry the chicken for 5 minutes until browned. Add the water, bring to the boil, cover and simmer gently for 15 minutes. Allow to cool in the pan.

remove the chicken and cut it into strips, reserving the pan juices. Place the chicken in a bowl and stir in the herbs, nuts and reserved juices.

cut the top from the loaf and scoop out the middle, leaving a 2.5 cm/1 inch thick shell. (You could make breadcrumbs from the filling and freeze for later use, if you like.)

spoon half the chicken into the hollow bread and carefully spread the pâté over the top. Add the remaining chicken and replace the bread lid. Wrap the loaf tightly in clingfilm, weigh down with a heavy object and chill in the refrigerator overnight. Cut into wedges to serve.

Serves 12
Preparation time: *20 minutes, plus marinating and chilling*
Cooking time: *20 minutes*

Baby Corn, Spring Onion and Coriander Salad

Crunchy little corn cobs in a dressing of spring onion, coriander and soy sauce make a memorable salad.

500 g/1 lb baby corn cobs, trimmed
2 tablespoons sesame seeds
6 spring onions, finely sliced
50 g/2 oz fresh coriander, chopped
50 ml/2 fl oz sunflower oil
2 teaspoons sesame oil
2 tablespoons freshly squeezed lime or lemon juice
1 tablespoon soy sauce
1–2 red chillies, deseeded and finely chopped (optional)
salt and pepper

bring a large saucepan of lightly salted water to the boil, add the corn and cook for 3–4 minutes, until it is just tender. Drain in a colander, refresh under cold water and then drain again.

meanwhile, place the sesame seeds in a dry frying pan. Heat, tossing, for 1–2 minutes, until browned. Remove from the heat and set aside.

mix together all the remaining ingredients except the sesame seeds in a salad bowl, add the corn and salt and pepper to taste and toss lightly. Sprinkle with the toasted sesame seeds and serve with crusty bread.

Serves 4–6
Preparation time: *20 minutes*
Cooking time: *3–4 minutes*

clipboard: Coriander, also known as Chinese parsley, has bright green lacy leaves and a deliciously intense flavour. It is particularly popular in Oriental styles of cookery.

Garden Vegetable Tart

Pastry

175 g/6 oz plain flour

25 g/1 oz ground hazelnuts

125 g/4 oz butter, chilled and diced

2 tablespoons grated Parmesan cheese

Filling

125 g/4 oz soft cheese with garlic and herbs

150 ml/¼ pint milk

2 eggs, beaten

500 g/1 lb cooked chopped vegetables (such as baby carrots, mangetout, leeks and asparagus)

125 g/4 oz cherry tomatoes

salt and pepper

mix the flour and hazelnuts in a bowl. Add the butter and rub in with the fingertips until the mixture resembles fine breadcrumbs. Stir in the Parmesan, then add enough cold water – about 2–3 tablespoons – to mix to a firm dough.

turn the dough out on a lightly floured surface and knead briefly. Roll out and line a 23 cm/9 inch pie plate. Prick the base all over with a fork, fill with crumpled foil and bake in a preheated oven, 200°C/400°F/Gas Mark 6, for 15 minutes, then lower the oven to 180°C/350°F/Gas Mark 4. Remove the foil and bake the pastry case for another 5 minutes. Remove from the oven and allow to cool. Leave the oven on.

to make the filling, combine the cheese, milk and eggs in a blender or food processor, and process until smooth. Season with salt and pepper. Fill the pastry case with the vegetables, then pour over the egg and cheese mixture. Bake the tart for 25 minutes, until the filling is firm.

Serves 6
Preparation time: *25 minutes*
Cooking time: *25 minutes*
Oven temperature: *200°C/400°F/Gas Mark 6*

Olive Focaccia

500 g/1 lb strong plain flour

2 teaspoons fast-action dried yeast

2 teaspoons sea salt, plus extra for scattering

½ teaspoon caster sugar

300 ml/½ pint warm water

50 g/2 oz black olives, pitted and roughly chopped

olive oil, to serve

Infused herb oil

1 rosemary sprig

1 thyme sprig

¼ red chilli

½ garlic clove

1 lemon rind strip

few fennel seeds, lighly bruised

2 peppercorns, bruised

4 tablespoons olive oil

to make the infused herb oil, place all the ingredients in a small, heavy-based saucepan and warm over a low heat for 20 minutes. Do not allow the oil to boil. Leave the oil to cool completely, then strain and set aside.

meanwhile, sift the flour into a bowl and stir in the yeast, salt and sugar. Make a well in the centre and gradually work in half the infused oil and the warm water, to form a soft dough. Turn out and knead on a lighly floured surface for 10 minutes.

cover the bowl with clingfilm and leave to rise in a warm place for about 1 hour until doubled in size.

knock back the dough, divide it in half and roll out each half to a 1 cm/½ inch thick oval. Transfer on to two greased baking sheets, cover with oiled clingfilm and set aside to rise for a further 30 minutes.

remove the clingfilm and press indentations all over the surface of each dough oval with your fingers. Scatter over a little sea salt and the olives, then drizzle over the remaining herb oil.

bake in a preheated oven, 220°C/425°F/Gas Mark 7, for 25–30 minutes until risen and golden. Cool slightly and serve warm cut into fingers with a bowl of olive oil for dipping.

Makes 2 oval breads
Preparation time: *15 minutes, plus rising*
Cooking time: *45–50 minutes*
Oven temperature: *220°C/425°F/Gas Mark 7*

Pan Bagnat Slices

Pan bagnat, a Niçoise stuffed bread, translates literally as 'wet bread'. A loaf is hollowed out, soaked with oil, stuffed and then put back together. It makes a great picnic dish, as well as a welcome snack.

2 red peppers
1 short French stick
1–2 garlic cloves, left whole
8 tablespoons extra virgin olive oil
1 tablespoon balsamic or sherry vinegar
4 ripe tomatoes, sliced
150 g/5 oz buffalo mozzarella cheese, sliced
12 large basil leaves
salt and pepper

grill the red peppers under a preheated grill for 15–20 minutes, turning frequently until charred on all sides. Transfer them to a plastic bag and leave until cool enough to handle.

meanwhile cut the French stick in half horizontally and scoop out and discard most of the middle, leaving a good 1 cm/½ inch thick edge. Set to one side to dry out slightly.

peel and deseed the peppers over a bowl to catch the juices and cut the flesh into quarters. Rub the insides of the French stick with the garlic and drizzle with the oil and vinegar.

arrange the peppers, tomato, mozzarella and basil in layers in one half of the French stick, seasoning with salt and pepper. Pour over the reserved pepper juices and any remaining olive oil.

replace the remaining half of the bread, wrap tightly in clingfilm and leave to chill overnight. Return to room temperature and cut the bread into 2 pieces to serve.

Serves 2
Preparation time: *30 minutes, plus chilling*
Cooking time: *15–20 minutes*

Watercress and Brie Quiche

125 g/4 oz plain flour
125 g/4 oz wholemeal flour
½ teaspoon salt
50 g/2 oz butter, softened
25 g/1 oz lard
about 5 tablespoons water
watercress sprigs, to garnish

Filling
300 g/10 oz ripe Brie cheese
300 ml/½ pint milk
125 g/4 oz watercress, trimmed
3 eggs, beaten
1 teaspoon mustard powder
pepper

sift the flours and salt into a bowl, adding the bran remaining in the sieve to the bowl. Rub in the fats until the mixture resembles breadcrumbs. Add just enough water to mix to a firm dough. Roll out on a lightly floured surface and use to line a 23 cm/9 inch loose-bottomed flan tin.

prick the base all over with a fork, fill with crumpled foil and bake in a preheated oven, 200°C/400°F/Gas Mark 6, for 10 minutes. Remove from the oven and lower the temperature to 180°C/350°F/Gas Mark 4.

meanwhile, remove the rind from the Brie. Dice the cheese, place in a saucepan with the milk and stir over a low heat until blended. Remove from the heat, stir in the watercress, beaten eggs and mustard and season with pepper to taste. Pour into the flan case and cook in the oven for 35 minutes. Allow to cool slightly before removing from the tin, then serve garnished with watercress.

Serves 6
Preparation time: *25 minutes*
Cooking time: *50 minutes*
Oven temperature: *200°C/400°F/Gas Mark 6*

Chocolate and Praline Terrine

A chocolate lover's fantasy – dense, rich and dark!

375 g/12 oz dark chocolate, broken into squares
2 tablespoons water
175 ml/6 fl oz double cream
75 g/3 oz unsalted butter
1–2 tablespoons rum
75 g/3 oz candied peel (optional)

Praline
125 g/4 oz sugar
125 g/4 oz whole blanched almonds

grease a 20 x 10 cm/8 x 4 inch loaf tin and line with nonstick baking paper. Oil a baking sheet.

make the praline. Combine the sugar and almonds in a small heavy-based saucepan. Heat gently until the sugar melts, stirring frequently. Continue to cook, stirring occasionally, until the sugar turns a deep golden brown. Immediately remove from the heat and pour the mixture on to the oiled baking sheet, spreading it out. Leave to cool. When the praline is completely cold, crush it into small pieces with a rolling pin.

melt the broken chocolate with the water in a heatproof bowl over a saucepan of barely simmering water. Leave to cool slightly.

whip the cream in a bowl until it forms soft peaks. In a separate bowl, cream the butter until soft and fluffy, then slowly stir in the chocolate mixture, followed by the rum. Fold in the cream, crushed praline and the candied peel, if using. Pour the mixture into the lined loaf tin. Level the top, cover and place in the refrigerator for 2–3 hours.

unmould the terrine on to a plate and cut into thin slices. Serve seasonal fresh fruit as an accompaniment.

Serves 6–8
Preparation time: *15 minutes, plus chilling*

Barbecues

Spare Ribs *with Ginger*

1 kg/2 lb pork spare ribs

Sauce

2 spring onions, chopped
2 cloves garlic, finely sliced
2.5 cm/1 inch piece of fresh root ginger, shredded
1 tablespoon soy sauce
4 tablespoons clear honey
3 tablespoons lemon juice
2 tablespoons mango chutney
½ teaspoon ground ginger
1 tablespoon oil
2 tablespoons dry sherry

arrange the spare ribs on the barbecue grid 10 cm/4 inches above hot coals and cook for 15 minutes, turning occasionally.

put all the sauce ingredients in a pan over a low heat, gradually bring to the boil and cook for 1 minute.

remove the ribs from the barbecue and place in a shallow dish. Spoon the sauce over the ribs, and turn to cover them all well.

return to the barbecue and cook for 10–15 minutes, basting frequently.

serve hot or cold with a green salad.

Serves 4–6
Preparation time: *10 minutes*
Cooking time: *25–30 minutes*

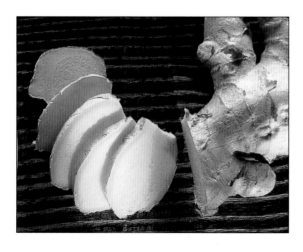

clipboard: Garlic has been in popular use for centuries as an important ingredient in many cuisines. It is also prized for its health-giving properties, being used to treat various ailments and to ward off evil spirits. Garlic is usually either crushed or, as in this recipe, finely sliced. Its pungent aroma and flavour immediately add character to any dish.

Coconut Butterfly Prawns

12 large raw tiger prawns, in their shells
2 garlic cloves, crushed
1 cm/½ inch piece of fresh root ginger, peeled and
very finely shredded
2 tablespoons freshly squeezed lime juice
1–2 red chillies, deseeded and finely chopped
150 ml/¼ pint coconut cream

to prepare the prawns, first remove the legs and cut off the heads with a small sharp knife. Holding a prawn with the back uppermost, slice along its length, from the thickest part toward the tail, cutting almost but not quite through. Carefully remove the dark vein that runs down its back.

gently press the prawn to flatten it out and make the butterfly shape. Repeat with the remaining prawns and rinse well under running water. Pat the prawns dry on kitchen paper and place them in a large flat dish.

mix the garlic, ginger, lime juice, chillies and coconut cream in a jug. Pour the mixture over the prawns, turning to coat them well. Cover the dish and marinate the prawns for 1–2 hours. Prepare 4 skewers and if using wooden skewers, soak them in cold water for about 30 minutes before use.

drain the prawns and thread them on to the skewers. Cook the prawns on a well-oiled barbecue grill over moderately hot coals for 5–6 minutes, turning once, until the flesh is opaque and just cooked. Serve at once.

Serves 4
Preparation time: *10 minutes, plus marinating*
Cooking time: *5–6 minutes*

Monkfish
Grilled with Fennel and Rosemary

500 g/1 lb ripe tomatoes, skinned

1 tablespoon balsamic vinegar

2 monkfish fillets, about 375 g/12 oz each, skinned

4 garlic cloves, cut into thin slivers

8 small rosemary sprigs

5 tablespoons olive oil

1 tablespoon lemon juice

salt and pepper

place the tomatoes in a blender or food processor and purée until smooth. Strain through a sieve into a bowl, season to taste with the vinegar, salt and pepper, then cover and set aside.

slice each fish fillet lengthways, almost but not quite all the way through, to make a pocket. Lay the garlic slivers down the length of the pocket in each fillet and top with rosemary sprigs. Add salt and pepper to taste. Reform both fillets and tie them with string at 1.5 cm/¾ inch intervals.

mix the olive oil and lemon juice in a shallow dish, large enough to hold both fillets. Add the monkfish, spoon the oil and lemon juice over the top, season with salt and pepper to taste, then cover and marinate for 1 hour, turning occasionally.

drain the monkfish and cook on an oiled barbecue grill, over moderately hot coals, for 15–20 mintues, basting frequently with the marinade, until the flesh is opaque and just cooked.

remove the string. Slice both fillets thinly. Serve on individual plates with the tomato sauce, warmed through, and crusty bread.

Serves 4

Preparation time: *30 minutes, plus marinating*

Cooking time: *15–20 minutes*

Black Bean Kebabs
with Mango Relish

125 g/4 oz dried black beans
3 tablespoons olive oil
1 onion, very finely chopped
1 garlic clove, crushed
1 red chilli, deseeded and finely chopped
½ teaspoon ground cumin
½ teaspoon ground coriander
1 tablespoon chopped fresh coriander
2 courgettes
24 mixed red and yellow cherry tomatoes

Mango relish
1 ripe mango
1 small onion, finely chopped
1 red chilli, deseeded and finely chopped
1 cm/½ inch piece of fresh root ginger, peeled and grated
salt and pepper

place the beans into a bowl, cover with cold water and soak overnight. Tip into a colander and rinse well under running water. Transfer to a saucepan, cover with fresh water and bring to the boil. Boil vigorously for 10 minutes, then lower the heat and simmer for 45–50 minutes until tender. Drain well.

to make the mango relish, peel the mango and cut the flesh away from the stone. Place in a bowl and mash lightly with a fork. Add the onion, chilli and ginger and mix well. Season with salt and pepper to taste.

heat 2 tablespoons of the oil in a frying pan. Add the onion, garlic and chilli, and cook gently for 5–10 minutes until the onion is soft but not coloured. Stir in the cumin and ground coriander and cook for a further 1–2 minutes. Turn the onion and spice mixture into a bowl, add the drained beans and fresh coriander and mash well. Divide the mixture into 24 and roll the portions into balls.

using a potato peeler, cut the courgette into long ribbons lengthways. Brush with the remaining oil. Thread the bean balls on to metal skewers, alternating with tomatoes and weaving the courgette strips in between.

cook the kebabs on a well-oiled barbecue grill over moderately hot coals for 4 minutes on each side. Serve with boiled rice and the mango relish.

Serves 4
Preparation time: *1 hour 20 minutes, plus soaking*
Cooking time: *8 minutes*

Spicy Beefburgers

1 kg/2 lb minced beef
2 tablespoons green peppercorns
1 tablespoon chopped thyme
2 teaspoons Worcestershire sauce
2 teaspoons French mustard
salt

To serve
8 burger buns
8 lettuce leaves
selection of relishes
1 onion, sliced
4 tomatoes, sliced

put the beef in a bowl and season well with salt. Stir in the peppercorns, thyme, Worcestershire sauce and mustard, and mix well. Divide into 8 portions and form into flat cakes.

cook the burgers on an oiled barbecue grill 10 cm/4 inches above the coals, or under a preheated moderate grill for 3–5 minutes on each side, according to taste.

cut the buns in half and toast the cut-side. Arrange a lettuce leaf on each bun base, top with a burger and relish. Arrange onion and tomato slices on top and replace the bun lid. Serve immediately.

Serves 4–8
Preparation time: *15 minutes*
Cooking time: *6–10 minutes*

clipboard: Line the base of your barbecue with heavy-duty foil. This will reflect the heat and will also make it easier to clean up afterwards. Hinged baskets are great for turning these homemade beefburgers.

Turkey Burgers
with Sun-dried Tomatoes and Tarragon

Richly seasoned turkey produces a mouthwatering burger.

8 sun-dried tomato halves in oil, drained and chopped

500 g/1 lb minced turkey

1 tablespoon chopped tarragon

½ red onion, finely chopped

¼ teaspoon paprika

¼ teaspoon salt

4 slices of smoked pancetta or rindless streaky bacon, cut in half

To serve
4 ciabatta rolls

shredded radicchio

shredded Cos lettuce

place the sun-dried tomatoes, turkey and tarragon in a liquidizer or food processor and blend until smooth. Spoon the mixture into a bowl and stir in the onion. Add the paprika and salt. Mix well, divide into 4 and shape into burgers. Stretch 2 strips of pancetta or bacon over each burger and secure with cocktail sticks soaked in water for 30 minutes.

cook the burgers on an oiled barbecue grill or under a preheated hot grill for 20–25 minutes, turning frequently. Serve at once in the ciabatta rolls with shredded lettuce.

Serves 4
Preparation time: *20 minutes*
Cooking time: *20–25 minutes*

clipboard: Tarragon is a delicately flavoured herb which is best used fresh. It goes particularly well with poultry, such as turkey or chicken. French tarragon is much more highly thought of than Russian tarragon as it has a much stronger scent and flavour.

Kofta Kebabs

This speciality from the Middle East consists of spiced minced lamb or beef pressed around skewers, grilled and served with a minty yogurt dip. If using wooden skewers, soak them in cold water for about 30 minutes before use to prevent them burning.

500 g/1 lb minced lamb or beef
1 onion, grated
50 g/2 oz pine nuts, roasted and chopped
1 tablespoon chopped oregano
½ teaspoon ground cumin
½ teaspoon ground coriander
salt and pepper

Yogurt dip

350 ml/12 fl oz Greek yogurt
3 tomatoes, skinned, seeded and chopped
1 tablespoon chopped mint
pinch of cayenne pepper
salt

first make the dip. Mix the yogurt, tomatoes and mint in a bowl. Season with a pinch each of cayenne and salt. Cover the bowl and place in the refrigerator until required.

place the minced lamb or beef in a food processor and mix to a smooth paste. Alternatively, pass through the finest blade of a mincer. Scrape into a bowl and stir in the onion, pine nuts, oregano and spices. Season with salt and pepper.

mould the mixture around 4 long skewers, forming it into sausage shapes or, alternatively, shape into balls. Place the skewers on an oiled barbecue grill over hot coals or under a preheated hot grill, and cook for about 10–12 minutes, turning frequently, until the meat is browned all over and cooked through.

remove the kebabs from the skewers, if liked, or serve one skewer per person, together with the yogurt dip. Pitta bread and a crisp salad of Cos lettuce are both appropriate accompaniments.

Serves 4
Preparation time: *20 minutes*
Cooking time: *10–12 minutes*

clipboard:Try fresh cucumber relish as an alternative to the yogurt dip.

Cinnamon-Spiced Chicken Wings
with Yellow Pepper Dip

Unusual, sweet and spicy, this is a delicious way to serve chicken wings.

8 large chicken wings

Marinade
1 garlic clove
5 cm/2 inch piece of fresh root ginger, peeled and chopped
juice and finely grated rind of 2 limes or 1 lemon
2 tablespoons light soy sauce
2 tablespoons groundnut oil
2 teaspoons ground cinnamon
1 teaspoon ground turmeric
2 tablespoons honey
salt, to taste
fresh coriander sprigs, to garnish

Yellow pepper dip
2 yellow peppers
4 tablespoons natural yogurt
1 tablespoon dark soy sauce
1 tablespoon chopped fresh coriander (optional)
pepper

place all the marinade ingredients in a liquidizer or food processor and blend until very smooth.

place the chicken in a bowl, pour over the marinade, toss, cover and leave to marinate for 1–2 hours.

make the yellow pepper dip: place the yellow peppers under a preheated grill for about 10 minutes, turning until well charred and blistered all over. Place in a plastic bag until cool, then peel, deseed and place the flesh in a liquidizer or food processor with the yogurt and blend until smooth. Pour into a bowl, add the soy sauce and season with pepper to taste; stir in the chopped coriander, if using, and set aside.

drain the chicken and cook on an oiled barbecue grill or under a preheated hot grill for 4–5 minutes on each side, basting with the remaining marinade. Garnish with coriander and serve with the dip.

Serves 4
Preparation time: *30 minutes, plus marinating*
Cooking time: *8–10 minutes*

Spiced Bananas

8 bananas, peeled
2 tablespoons lemon juice
8 tablespoons soft brown sugar
50 g/2 oz butter
1 teaspoon cinnamon

place each banana on a double piece of foil. Brush well with the lemon juice and sprinkle 1 tablespoon sugar on each.

cream together the butter and cinnamon and divide between the bananas, dotting along the top.

wrap each banana securely in the foil and cook on the barbecue grill, about 10 cm/4 inches above the coals, for 10 minutes. Unwrap and serve hot with Rum Mascarpone Cream (see below).

Serves 8
Preparation time: *10 minutes*
Cooking time: *10 minutes*

clipboard: To make a delicious Rum Mascarpone Cream to serve with the bananas, mix together 250 g/8 oz mascarpone cheese, 2 tablespoons rum and 1–2 tablespoons caster sugar, to taste. Chill until ready to serve.

Rum-Flambéed Pineapple Parcels

This is a simple and delicious dessert — and it's easy to omit the rum from children's portions.

1 ripe pineapple, peeled
50 g/2 oz butter
75 g/3 oz light muscovado sugar
4 tablespoons dark rum
50 g/2 oz pecan nuts, roasted and coarsely chopped
ice cream, crème fraîche or fromage blanc, to serve

cut the pineapple into 8 even slices, then remove the cores with a small pastry cutter to make rings.

cut out 4 double-thickness foil squares, each large enough to hold 2 pineapple rings in a loose parcel. Place 2 rings on each square.

melt the butter in a small pan, stir in the sugar and cook gently until the sugar has dissolved. Divide between the parcels, then bring the edges of the foil together and press to seal.

cook on a grill over moderately hot coals or under a preheated hot grill for 10–15 minutes.

open each package; spoon 1 tablespoon of rum into each and carefully ignite with a match. Scatter over the chopped pecans and serve at once with ice cream, crème fraîche or fromage blanc.

Serves 4
Preparation time: *15 minutes*
Cooking time: *10–15 minutes*

clipboard: Pecan nuts are native to America and are closely related to the walnut. The flavour is rich and buttery and is brought out by roasting. Because pecans have such a high oil content, they can soon turn rancid, so store them in a cool, dark, dry place and use within 6 months.

Index

Acknowledgments

Special photography by Jean Cazals
All other photos:
Octopus Publishing Group Limited / William Lingwood, Jean Cazals, Chris Crofton, Philip Dowell, Laurie Evans, Sue Jorgensen, Graham Kirk, Sandra Lane, Fred Mancini, Hilary Moore, Vernon Morgan, Roger Philips, Roger Stowell, Clive Streeter, Philip Webb, Paul Williams

Home economist
Marie-Ange Lapierre
Jacket home economist
Sunil Vijayakar